TILE DESIGNS

MORE THAN 100 READY-TO-USE TILING PATTERNS

TILE DESIGNS

MORE THAN 100 READY-TO-USE TILING PATTERNS **Leila Adam**

FIREFLY BOOKS

A FIREFLY BOOK

Published by Firefly Books Ltd. 2009

First published in 2009 in New Zealand by David Bateman Ltd.,
30 Tarndale Grove, Albany, Auckland, New Zealand

Publisher Cataloging-in-Publication Data (U.S.)

Adam, Leila.
    Tile designs : more than 100 ready-to-use tiling patterns / Leila Adam.
[160] p. : col. photos. ; cm.
Summary: Instructions and ideas for creating tile designs based on the principle of tessellation using off-the-shelf tiles. Designs for small and large spaces, indoors and outdoors, floors and walls, along with brief instructions for laying ceramic tiles.
ISBN-13: 978-1-55407-485-3 (pbk.)
ISBN-10: 1-55407-485-1 (pbk.)
1. Tiles – Themes, motives.   I. Title.
745.4 dc22   NK4670.A336 2009

A CIP record is available for this title from Library and Archives Canada.

Published in the United States by Firefly Books (U.S.) Inc.
P.O. Box 1338, Ellicott Station
Buffalo, New York 14205

Published in Canada by Firefly Books Ltd.
66 Leek Crescent
Richmond Hill, Ontario L4B 1H1

Book design: Julie McDermid/Punaromia
Printed in China through Colorcraft Ltd, Hong Kong

Contents

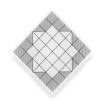

Introduction

This book offers an opportunity to make creative patterns with tiles, without the specialized techniques required for mosaic work or tile painting and glazing. It is about using the tiles that can be bought in any flooring store and laying them in the usual way, but with the added benefit of creating an interesting pattern. No extra skill is required besides normal tile-laying techniques. (These are outlined on pages 8–13.) The key concept is that tiles of different colors are laid according to a plan that creates a pattern.

Where can one look for inspiration in designing interesting tile patterns? In fact, any design that can be envisaged as being based on a square grid can be used. If a design can be translated onto a square grid, it can be represented in tiles. For example, one could take a plan that would normally be used in cross-stitch and make a tile pattern with it, using a square tile to represent each cross. Quilting patterns with geometric shapes can be used in a similar way.

Tessellation lends itself very well to tile patterning. Tessellation is the mathematical art of fitting a shape together continuously, leaving no gaps. If a tessellation pattern can be fitted onto a square grid, it can be represented in tiles. The most often used tile pattern, the checkerboard pattern, is in fact a tessellation of squares. This book explores the use of tessellation in tile pattern designing.

Interesting patterns can be found in many traditional cultures. Decorative work on masonry, fabrics, pottery, basketwork, glass and other traditionally used surfaces can provide inspiration for a tiling pattern. Zigzags, woven lines and geometric designs can be lifted from traditional artwork and used in a whole new way. It takes just a little practice to train the eye to spot the possibilities.

The Middle East provides a rich source of traditional patterns. One reason for this is the fact that its dominant religion, Islam, discourages realistic representations in art. Art has had religious connections in all cultures, and while other societies developed artistic genres showing lifelike representations of gods and traditional stories, Islamic art was, for the most part, completely abstract. This book explores many examples of traditional designs from the Middle East.

The idea for this book came about from a flooring project for the entranceway to a public building. The floor was to be tiled in a way that would produce a pleasant visual focus for people entering. But, being a community project, it was undesirable to involve the extra costs and expertise associated with producing a mosaic for the entrance. A simpler idea was needed, and so we sat down with square grid math paper and started to experiment with shapes. Once we began, we realized the possibilities were endless! We also realized that many classic geometric designs that are usually produced using different media could be very easily produced in tiles. Soon, drawing tile patterns became an obsessive hobby, and the *Tile Designs* book was born.

How to lay ceramic floor tiles

This section covers laying floor tiles. If you intend tiling both walls and the floor, do the walls first. The same basic steps and principles of laying ceramic floor tiles apply to various other types of floor tile. (For further information on laying tiles, visit your local tile dealer in-store or online.)

Materials	Tools	
▪ Tiles	▪ Chalk / chalk line	▪ Safety glasses
▪ Leveling compounds	▪ Adhesive applicator	▪ Pencil
▪ Tile adhesive	▪ Notched trowel or spreader	▪ Scoring tool
▪ Plastic tile spacers	▪ Measuring tape or folding rule	▪ Cloth
▪ Floor tile grout	▪ Straight edge / level	▪ Sponge
▪ Flexible grout sealant (silicone or water-based)	▪ Tile nippers / tile cutter / diamond wheel cutter	

Choosing the right tiles

Tile floor covering is excellent for its natural look, durability and ease of care. Tiles work well in areas with high foot traffic, and they are especially good for entry areas.

Select tiles appropriate for the area. Tile hardness can vary to suit the amount of likely foot traffic. Check with the supplier.

- Entryways require hard, abrasion-resistant, moisture-proof tiles.
- Bathrooms, laundry and other wet areas need moisture-proof, nonslip tiles.
- Some tiles can be used only indoors or only outdoors. Check with the supplier.
- Floor tiles vary in size and thickness, usually ½ to ¾ inches (13–19 mm) thick, in squares measuring 4 x 4 inches (100 x 100 mm) up to 24 x 24 inches (600 x 600 mm) or more. Wall tiles are thinner, in squares usually 3 x 3 inches (75 x 75 mm) up to 6 x 6 inches (150 x 150 mm).

(Also see the information on tile types on page 13.)

Buying tiles

Tiles are usually sold in packs, and the size of the tiles and number of tiles per pack will determine the surface area that the tiles will cover. Work out the area to be covered and round up to get the correct number of tiles required.

- Check tiles for faults before laying them.

1. Preparing the base surface

- **Concrete:** Ceramic tiles can be laid directly onto a concrete surface. (Tiling should be carried out at least three months after concrete is poured. The concrete should be dry, without residual dampness. If a rubber mat left overnight is moist underneath the next morning, the concrete is still not dry.) The base concrete surface must be level and sound. Pronounced dips, hollows and joints can be filled and leveled using underlay sheeting or leveling compounds. Remove all wax, grease or oil from the surface with an appropriate cleaner.
- **Wood:** To lay tiles on a wooden floor, it should first be strengthened and leveled with ½ inch (13 mm) thick plywood. Ensure nail heads are level with or below the plywood surface.

For best results choose a tile adhesive that is suited to the surface that you are laying the tiles on.

2. Positioning the tiles

a. Mark a chalk line on the floor down the center of the room parallel with the wall that will give the best layout.

b. Place the first row of loose tiles (without adhesive) down this line. (The design plan will influence which tiles you begin with.) Line up the tiles so that they look straight as you enter the room. *(See photo 1.)*

c. Work outward toward the walls, creating a space between the tiles with plastic tile spacers. Any gap between ⅛ and ½ inches (3–13 mm) can be used. Often a wide gap of ¼ inch (6 mm) or more may be more attractive than a narrow gap. *(See photo 2.)*

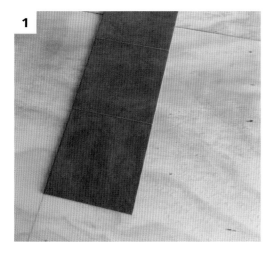

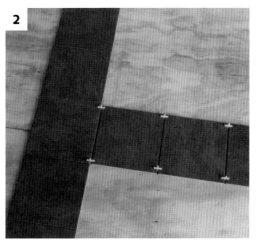

d. If the final line of tiles before the edge of the area is less than half a tile wide, adjust all the tiles across until the gap is at least half a tile wide. This avoids difficult small cuts. *(See photo 3.)*

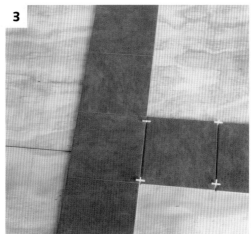

3. Cutting tiles

Use safety glasses when cutting tiles.

Using tools

Floor tiles are generally thicker than wall tiles and so harder to cut. It is advisable to use a professional tile cutting tool (diamond/wet saw) for these tiles.

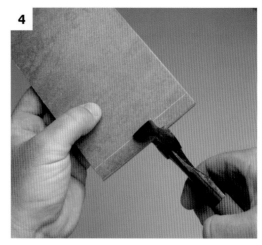

- **Using tile nippers:** Center the cutting blade on the scored line. Exert pressure by squeezing the handles together. Use your free hand to hold the side of the tile you will be using. *(See photo 4.)*

- **Using a tile cutter:** Measure and mark the cutting line on the tile. Align this mark with the cutting guide on the tile cutter. Supporting the tile to keep it level, lower the cutting wheel onto the edge of the tile. Push it away from you with firm pressure. When you've rolled the cutting wheel to the far end, push down on the handle to split the tile. *(See photo 5.)*

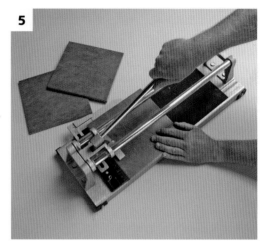

- **Using a wet saw:** Measure and mark the cutting line on the tile. Align this mark with the cutting guide on the tile cutter. Supporting the tile to keep it level, move it toward the blade. Move the tile slowly to avoid overheating and cracking it. Don't force it through; let the saw do the work. *(See photo 6.)*

By hand with a glass cutter

- Mark the glazed surface. Place a ruler or straight edge along the line and firmly score the surface with a glass cutter. With the scored line facing up, position the tile over a matchstick or nail that is in line with the cut. Press down firmly on both sides; this will result in a clean break. The scored tile can also be broken by pressing down against a table edge. *(See photo 7.)*

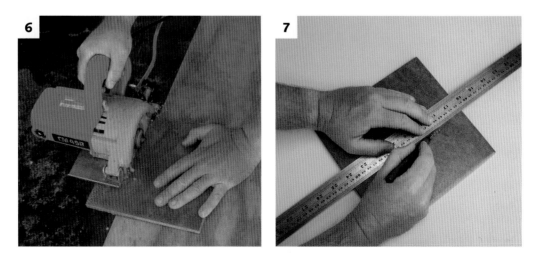

Cutting shapes

- To cut half circles, scratch the shape on the glazed surface with a glass cutter. Hold the tile as closely as possible to where the cut is being made. Next nip off very small pieces at a time with a sharp cutter, then nip off very small pieces with a sharp pair of pincers until the correct fit is achieved. Smooth off sharp edges with a tile file.
- When marking tiles to cut an irregular shape, use a paper or cardboard template to mark the cutting line on the tile. *(See photo 8.)*

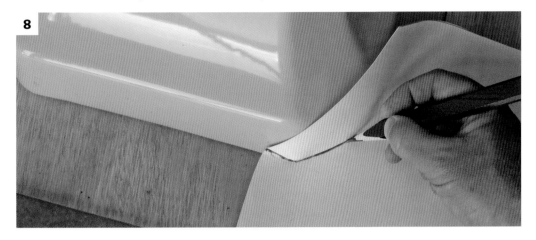

8

Smoothing off edges

- Use tile nippers or pliers to nibble off the jagged edge of a broken tile. Use a round file to smooth the edges of areas that have been nibbled away.

4. Straight cutting at edges

Place a whole tile on top of the last complete tile that was adhered in place. Hold another whole tile so that it touches the wall. Mark a line along the lower tile. The off-cut from the lower tile will fit into the gap. *(See photo 9.)*

5. Laying tiles

- Remove loose tiles from floor. Check the information on the adhesive pack. Apply adhesive to an area of about 1 square yard (1 sq. m) at a time or it will begin to harden before the tiles are applied to it. Apply adhesive to the floor or wall with a notched spreader or trowel. *(See photo 10.)*
- Start laying tiles at your chalk line in the center of the floor. Push each tile downward in place onto the adhesive until it oozes out at the corners (avoid sliding tile). Remove any excess adhesive.

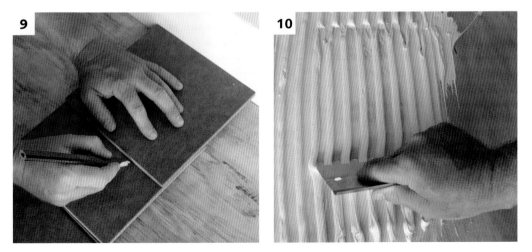

9

10

- Use tile spacers between every tile and ensure that these are pushed down fully to enable you to grout over them. *(See photo 11.)*
- Every so often use a straight edge or level to ensure all tiles are lying flat. Remove any tiles above or below the level of adjoining ones and adjust adhesive depth. Do not leave this task for too long or it will be impossible to remove the tiles. Following your design, fix all whole tiles, then cut and fix the tiles around the edge. *(See photo 12.)*

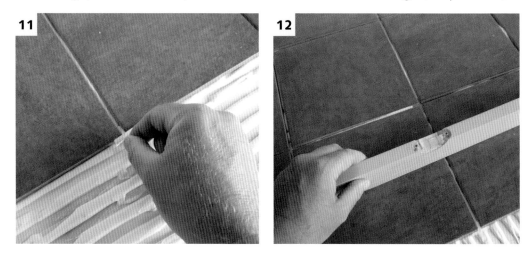

6. Grouting

Grout only when the adhesive is completely dry, about a 24-hour period. Using waterproof grout, force the mixture between the gaps in the tiles with a grout spreader, working in a diagonal fashion across the tile gaps. Remove any surface grout regularly with a damp cloth. *(See photo 13.)*

7. Cleaning

Using a clean, wet sponge, wash out and wipe away any remaining grout until the joints are smooth and level with the tiles. After 30 minutes of drying, a hazy grout film will appear. Wipe this away with a soft cloth. *(See photo 14.)*

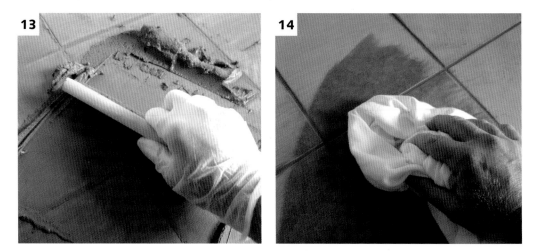

8. Sealing

At least 72 hours after the grout is set and dry, apply a silicone or water-based flexible grout sealer to the joint gaps (removing any drips on your tiles with a rag). The sealer will make the grouted gaps more resistant to water and mildew, and it will help keep dirt out of the joints. *(See photo 15.)*

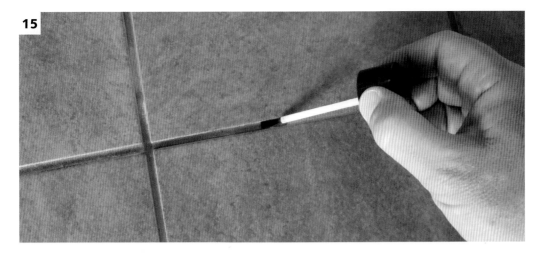

15

Do not wash your new tile floor for at least a week after installation.

Types of tiles

Brick	Available in earth-tone colors, brick tiles are good for an informal or rustic look. They should be treated with a stain-resistant sealer. Floor brick is normally used in outdoor settings, such as patios.
Cement	Made in molds then fired or dried naturally. Color may be added. Sealing is required after installation for moisture and stain resistance. Primarily used indoors because they're not frost-proof.
Ceramic	Made from clay or other minerals and kiln fired. Clay tiles are either glazed or unglazed: **Glazed:** Color is added to the tile after firing. The glasslike surface is bonded to the tile. Glazing allows brighter colors and more color choices and adds stain resistance. The smooth surface of glazed tiles means they are used mostly on walls and countertops. **Unglazed:** The pigment or natural color is present during firing and is part of the tile itself. Unglazed tiles need sealing for moisture-proofing and stain resistance.
Mosaic	Porcelain or ceramic mosaic tiles (glazed or unglazed) are usually small (2 inches [50 mm] square or smaller). Can be installed individually or purchased pre-mounted on mesh or paper sheets.
Pavers	Pavers are thinner than brick tiles. Shale-based pavers are used for patios as well as interior floors. Like unglazed ceramic tiles, pavers require sealing for moisture-proofing and stain resistance.
Porcelain	Clay is fired at a very high temperature, making a dense tile (which is more resistant to moisture).
Quarry	Quarry tile is an unglazed ceramic tile, durable and relatively inexpensive, usually available in earth colors of red and orange. It requires sealing for wet areas.
Saltillo	Saltillo (or Mexican tile) is air dried rather than kiln dried, which means the tile is somewhat softer and less durable, but it gives the tile a look that is unique. When used indoors a sealer is required.
Terra-cotta	Terra-cotta (or clay) tiles have a natural, earthy look. Being absorbent, they need to be treated for indoor use.
Terrazzo	Terrazzo tiles are made with stone or marble chips embedded in cement. The polished surface makes a durable floor material.

Chapter 1

Tiling patterns

Tiles are a practical form of floor or wall covering. They are durable, easy to clean and visually appealing. Tiles are becoming an increasingly popular option for both indoor and outdoor areas. Homes and workplaces alike are increasingly being decorated with tiles.

Tiling can be a powerful home-decorating medium. Not only are tiles hard wearing, they are also beautiful. When laid in a single color they can harmonize everything in a room and produce a cool, serene effect. On the other hand, tiles laid in different colors can add interest to a plain room. Because tiling is done in basic units of the same shape, and because each piece can be chosen in a different color, a tiled floor or wall can become like a canvas on which to create a work of art.

What happens when one chooses tiles and wishes to lay them in an interesting and original way? There are enormous possibilities to create stunning patterns, with very little extra effort in the laying process. A tiling pattern will give increased pleasure when viewing the area, as well as provide something unique that reflects your own creativity.

This book provides an inspirational look at the artistic possibilities for tiling patterns. Chapters group designs into similar types and provide structure to the enormous variety of effects that can be produced. The collection of over a hundred designs can also be used as a pattern library to choose a design that will soon grace your floor or wall. Use the patterns as they are or alter them according to your own inspiration. The possibilities are only limited by the imagination!

Each drawing displayed represents a unique geometric design. Most patterns are made up of a basic unit of the design that can be repeated and extended indefinitely. When a basic unit is repeated to fill a space, it is exciting to see the new geometric relationships created. The patterns can also be truncated, so that only a part of the design is chosen. Many of the drawings in the book are accompanied by photographs of the artwork or traditional decorations which inspired them.

Tiles are generally square or rectangular in shape. Paving stones, which can be viewed in a similar way to floor tiles, often have more varied shapes. The shape of the tile dictates the kind of pattern that can be produced. Most commercially available flooring and wall tiles are square. Because of their shape, square tiles can produce patterns that are balanced and symmetrical. Many straight-edged geometrical shapes can be represented. Any shape that is built up of 45-degree and 90-degree angles can be produced with square tiles.

For simplicity, all the patterns produced here use only whole square tiles or diagonally cut tiles. There is no need to cut tiles any smaller than this for any pattern in this book.

To create most of the patterns in this book, some tiles will need to be cut on the diagonal. To do this, mark in the diagonal line. Then follow the tile cutting instructions given in the previous section (on page 10), using either a glass cutter, tile cutter or wet saw. You will need to make two cuts across the tile, removing a tile spacer's width of tile so that when laid with grout between them, the two halves form a square. A machine (wet saw) will probably give a neater result, especially on the more sharply pointed end of the resulting triangle. This diagonal cutting can be tricky and time-consuming, but a tiling retailer will usually be able to provide a professional cutting facility for a batch of tiles.

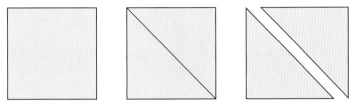

Whole square tile   Diagonally cut tile producing two triangles

Tiles are laid in a two-dimensional plane using a grid that represents the repeated shape of the tile. For patterning purposes, this grid becomes the canvas upon which to produce a design. All designs must begin with a blank canvas, so one is provided below. This grid, and those at the back of the book, can be copied and used as a tile pattern "sketch pad."

1.1 Blank Square Tile Grid

Practical considerations in patterned tiling

When considering the use of a pattern in a flooring or wall situation, it is important to consider the effects of tile size and color. Color combinations and their overall effect will have a big impact on the finished product. Placing different-colored tiles together to view their combined effects is advisable before making a final color choice.

Commercially available tiles are often subtly different in size and texture, so it is usually best to choose different colors from the same tile range. Choosing tiles from different ranges and with different textures might produce an undesirable hodgepodge effect, rather than a design that looks unified and well planned. Tiles that are just slightly different in size can also be a problem, as they may not produce clean lines when laid. The eye is remarkably good at seeing these small anomalies, and they can spoil the effect of a dramatic design. A tiling professional will be able to give advice about how well the chosen tiles will fit together.

The colors used in the drawings in this book are relatively unimportant and are mainly there to show the effect of contrasts and to display the pattern clearly. Patterns have usually been limited to using two or three color combinations. Simplicity is a key factor in ensuring that a design has maximum impact. For example, there is nothing more striking than a flooring pattern produced in black and white. Having said this, there is nothing to stop you from choosing any number of colors for your own use of the patterns represented in this book.

One should keep in mind that most commercially available flooring tiles are colored in natural earth tones. Natural tones are quite relaxing to the senses. If less contrasting, naturally toned colors are chosen to render a design, the pattern produced will be more subtle in impact.

Wall tiles, on the other hand, are often very colorful. If choosing a pattern for a feature wall, the result of making the design in bright, contrasting colors can be quite spectacular.

The size of the finished product in a tiling project will depend on the size of the tiles used. Many floor tiles are somewhere between 12 inches (30 cm) and 18 inches (45 cm) square. When choosing a pattern it is important to measure the area to be tiled, as well as the size of each tile. A calculation of the square feet (or square meters) of floor area and knowing how many tiles of your choice are needed to cover, say, 10 square feet (1 sq. m, approximately) will help you establish how many tiles are required and whether your chosen pattern will be appropriate. A flooring store or a tiling professional will be able to help with this.

Of course, any pattern can be truncated so that just a part of it is used, so areas whose finished shapes are not square can be filled in this way. We can also use part of a different design to fill an oddly shaped area in the scheme. Many of the designs here represent one unit of a pattern that can be repeated endlessly in any direction. This means that very large areas can also be catered for.

The patterns in this book are generally presented in an 18 x 18 square grid. Based on tiles which are 12 inches (30 cm) square in size, this represents a finished tile pattern size of 18 feet x 18 feet = 324 square feet (5.4 m x 5.4 m = 29.2 sq. meters) in area.

Wall tiling using smaller tiles will, of course, produce different-sized finished products. For example, 6-inch (15 cm) square tiles will result in a 9-foot x 9-foot = 81-square-foot (2.7 m x 2.7 m = 7.3 sq. m) wall area for the 18 x 18 grid patterns. Thus, a complex pattern might be able to be represented in a relatively small wall area.

In many cases, the patterns are more striking when viewed from afar or when made with small tiles to produce the same effect as seeing the pattern from a distance. To appreciate this, try viewing the pages of the book from across the room or in a mirror.

Other uses for square grid patterns

Although the focus is on tile laying, a square grid pattern can be used in other ways, such as for patchwork or cross-stitch projects. Because the patterns are based on squares, they are easy to copy and reproduce in colors and materials of one's own choosing.

A few examples of simple art work that can be produced with the help of square grid patterns follow:

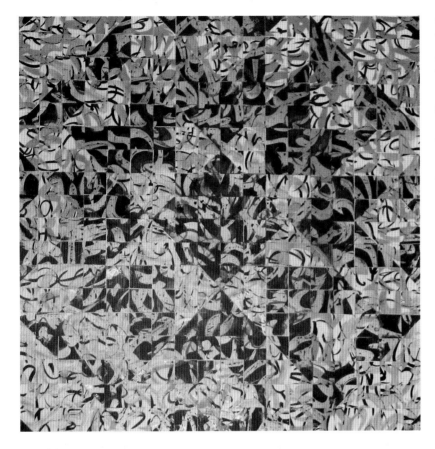

Cardboard Collage, L. Adam

The Cardboard Collage was produced by decoratively painting two sheets of card, one based in red, the other in yellow. Then the sheets were cut into squares and half squares and glued onto a thick card base with a square grid penciled onto it. The design used is drawing 8.1.

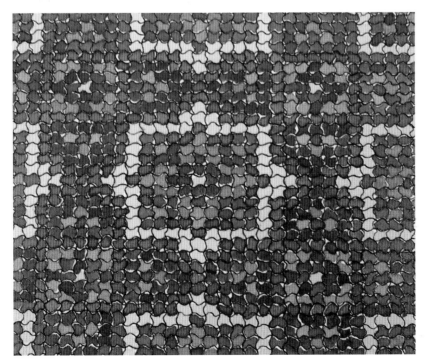

Acrylic miniature painting, L. Adam

This whole square miniature painting in acrylics was made using drawing 11.17. The edges of the squares were distorted to produce added interest and less rigidity to the design.

Chapter 2

Making square grid designs

Sometimes flooring stores have inspiring displays of tiling designs, but where does one go to find more of these? Most books about tiles focus on making tiles, making mosaics or on painting or glazing tile surfaces. These produce beautiful effects but require more specialized work.

On the other hand, a design based on a square grid is accessible and can be produced by anyone simply by using store-bought square floor tiles and laying them in the usual way. Currently, there are not many ready-made tiling designs to be found, although this book provides a start. So how does one begin to draw an original design that can be reproduced as a tiling pattern?

To produce designs to use for tiling, we need to look at patterns in the environment around us with fresh eyes, to "think outside the square" – or rather, in this case, to "think *in* squares!"

The fun part is often in seeing a traditional decoration or piece of craftwork and conceiving a grid design inspired by it. This requires a little practice. In this chapter we will examine four different examples of art or craftwork and see how to turn each into a square grid pattern.

Traditional designs

Consider the mother-of-pearl design on the traditional Egyptian hand drum pictured below.

2.1 Diamond Border

The border pattern of squares with diamonds could be rendered in tiles by expanding each square to be represented by four tiles. This allows the diamonds to be shown easily. One line of the resulting border design would then look like this sketch.

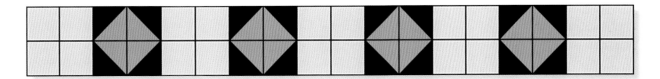

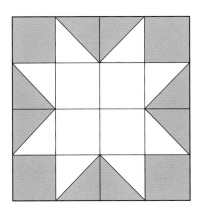

2.2 Classic Eight-Pointed Star

The star design at the center of the drum decoration can also be represented easily in tiles. The clue to knowing whether it will fit into a square grid is in noting that it is an eight-pointed star. Eight-pointed stars can be represented by squares, whereas most six-pointed stars can be represented only by a triangular grid.

The eight-pointed star in the photo is a classic design that is found at the center of many drawings in this book. It is one of the two basic eight-pointed star designs that can easily be exhibited in square tiles.

To render the star in the photograph into a square grid pattern, we need to rotate it a little. It can then be represented by this 4 × 4 tile pattern.

2.3 Egyptian Drum Pattern

Next we consider the diamonds surrounding the star. They need to become squares in order to fit into the grid, and four of them become fatter than the original design. The red line detailing on the outer row of squares needs to be left out, and the shapes are tilted at a different angle. Thus, the resulting grid design could look like this sketch.

2.4 Altered Drum Pattern

Once we have a basic design such as the one in drawing 2.3, we can use it to think up variations. We might decide to extract or delete parts of the pattern to make it simpler or change some of the coloring to highlight one feature and soften another. The altered drum design in this drawing is an example.

We can get inspiration for a border pattern from a basic design such as this altered drum pattern. Depending on how wide we want the border to be, we can extract a long section and repeat it lengthwise. The drum pattern could be used in this way to produce at least five different border patterns, including diagonal ones. Of course, the whole design could be repeated lengthwise as well, to produce a wider border. A few of the possible border patterns that can be lifted from the design above follow.

2.5 Diamond and Square Border

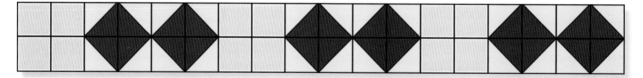

2.6 Flower and Diamonds Border

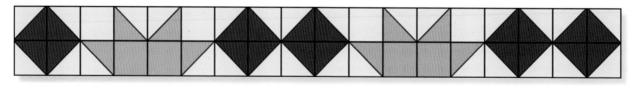

2.7 Eight-Star with Cross-Hatch Border

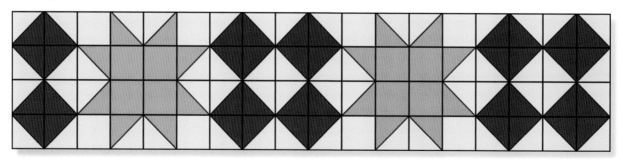

Finally, we might consider using the pattern as a basic unit and repeating it many times. This can have surprising effects when new angles and shapes are formed as the edges of the blocks interplay with one another.

This was one of the aspects of geometric design that fascinated early Islamic artists. Once a repeated design is produced, the eyes marvel at the total visual effect of it. In religious terms, it becomes an apt artistic metaphor for individuals standing in worship en masse and together producing a strong and united society. Equally, it can remind the viewer of all the separate units of God's creation that come together to make a beautiful and harmonious whole.

2.8 Eight-Star Checkerboard

This is the first drum design repeated four times.

Cross-stitch designs

2.9 Cross-Stitch Plan of Flower Motif

The photo shows part of a traditional Palestinian cross-stitch design on a dress.
Part of this design is represented as the cross-stitching plan (at right).

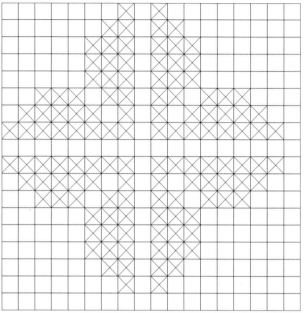

2.10 Cross-Stitch Flower

In order to make the traditional pattern into a square grid design suitable for tiling, one simply
needs to convert each cross into a square. Note that this will produce a tiling pattern that uses
only whole squares. No diagonal lines will be involved. Any cross-stitch design can be converted
to a tiling pattern in this way, as long as you have enough space to create it!

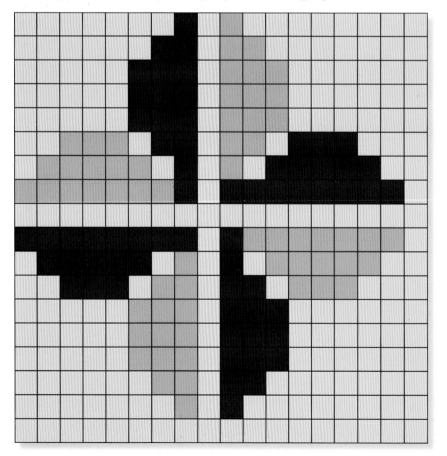

Tessellation patterns

Tessellation is the art of fitting many repetitions of the same shape together to fill a flat plane completely, with no gaps. It is a subject that will be dealt with in more depth in the following chapters. Here the focus is on viewing a ready-made tessellation pattern and seeing if it can translate onto a square tile grid.

A great source of ready-made tessellation patterns is the work of the famed Dutch artist M.C. Escher. Escher loved tessellation and based much of his work on it. He traveled around Europe making sketches that inspired his art and, in the process, visited the Alhambra in Spain. Here he saw the many murals of repeating geometric designs made by Muslim artists. It was after this visit that his fascination with tessellation really exploded into a proliferation of marvelous works of art.

How do we turn our favorite Escher drawing into a tiling pattern? Basically, one tries to mentally place a square grid over the top of the picture and then sketch it as accurately as possible, using the straight and diagonal lines of the grid. Sketching out the design on square math paper can be helpful.

2.11 Escher's Flying Birds

For example, this process was carried out on Escher's flying bird drawing, shown in the photo (at right). An adaptation of the drawing to fit a square grid produces the tiling pattern pictured (at left). This is not the only result that could have been produced, as it is a rather fluid process. Notice how the new pattern requires three colors to display it clearly, compared with the original pattern which needed only two. (For more Escher adaptations see chapter 4.)

M. C. Escher's "Symmetry Drawing E106."

Islamic geometric designs

Islamic art and architecture provides such a rich source of patterning ideas that it deserves special mention. Over the centuries, Muslim geometric artists and craftspeople shared, copied and bounced their geometric designs around until they had spread through all the countries from southern Europe right across to Southeast Asia. Thus, for example, today we still marvel at the complex geometric work on such architectural wonders as the Alhambra in Spain and the Taj Mahal in India.

Since Islam discourages the representation of people and animals in art, creativity for Muslim artists took a unique route. By creating a seemingly endless geometric pattern, the artist conveyed to the viewer a sense of infinity that held great spiritual significance. It was a way of representing the infinite nature and perfection of God's creation, and it gave the idea of vastness and complexity that reminded the viewer about the uncountable things God has created. The symmetry and satisfaction of patterns that fit together perfectly also conveyed the perfection with which God made everything in nature interact and work in harmony together. Moreover, viewing these complex patterns has a surprisingly relaxing effect on the mind, and so their use was especially appropriate for decorating mosques and private homes.

Many patterns in this book have been derived from architectural decorations on Muslim buildings, such as mosques, palaces and houses. The Middle East abounds in beautiful geometric grilles, lattices and surface designs made in many materials. Carved wood, iron grilles, plasterwork and bricks are among the most common materials used. Tiles were sometimes used in this way, though usually as whole-tile patterns using very small tiles to produce the effect of a mosaic.

Much of this book is devoted to translating such classic Islamic geometric designs into square grid patterns. This makes the designs immediately accessible for use in tiling and provides a practical way in which these beautiful patterns can grace our working and living spaces. Wherever possible, the origin of these designs has been noted.

If you wish to make a tile design that attempts to achieve an authentic tiled Middle Eastern look, choose colors such as black, olive green, turquoise, tan, cream, powder blue and royal blue.

The photos below and opposite show a typical Islamic geometric lattice, followed by a breakdown of how this lattice can become a tiling pattern (drawings 2.12 to 2.14).

The clue to knowing whether or not a design such as this one can become a tiling design is to look at the angles. If the pattern seems to contain angles of 45 and 90 degrees, it is likely to make a successful square grid pattern. Shapes that are related to the numbers four and eight also give positive clues. We see all these features in the pattern

shown in the photos. It is made up of interlocking squares and octagons and has a background of parallel lines that are at right angles to one another.

Many geometric designs, on the other hand, are based on triangles, especially equilateral ones. Unfortunately these designs cannot be translated onto a square grid.

To make this lattice pattern into a tiling design, use a blank square grid and try to copy the pattern, using the least amount of squares possible. Analyze the pattern to see what the repeating unit is. If the angles in the original design are not exactly 45 or 90 degrees, the pattern will be altered in your drawing, but in some cases this can still produce a pleasing design.

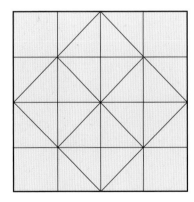

2.12 Diamond Lattice
Building the pattern slowly, the diamonds in the lattice above would be rendered on the square grid as shown.

2.13 Diamond Lattice with Octagon
The octagons would then be added, surrounding the diamond. Four connecting lines are also inserted in each corner.

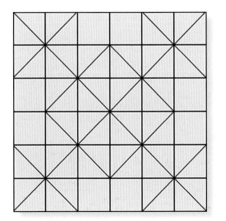

2.14 Dubai Wall Lattice (1)
Now we have found the basic unit of the design, and this can be repeated to form the whole pattern.

2.15 Dubai Wall Lattice (2)

Finally, color is put into the design. The colors need to be chosen in a way that will bring out the pattern clearly. In this case, to show all the shapes in the original lattice, we need a minimum of four colors. Sometimes the result is surprising, as in this case, where a fairly straightforward lattice pattern became a complex tiling pattern requiring more than two colors. This drawing shows one possible color rendering of the design.

2.16 Dubai Wall Lattice (3)

How a design is colored affects its appearance profoundly. First, there is an effect created by the interplay of the colors placed next to each other. Then there is the change that can occur in a pattern if the placing and number of colors used alters. The same pattern can be colored differently to simplify the shapes, emphasizing some and eliminating others. Thus, with a different color rendering this pattern could appear as shown.

Now we have covered some of the skills needed to create interesting tiling designs and, as always, skills improve with practice. Even just appreciating what is involved in creating a tile design will increase the enjoyment of viewing other patterns. You may choose to use any of the designs presented in this book as they stand or, armed with some of the skills presented here, alter them in your own creative manner.

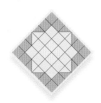

Chapter 3

Tessellation for tiles

The subject of tessellation was touched on in the previous chapter when looking at the work of artist M.C. Escher. The next four chapters deal further with tessellation in the context of square grids. First, a very basic notion of tessellation is introduced. Then we show a different way to create tessellated designs by presenting a standard mathematical process, often taught in elementary schools. This is a powerful method that allows us to turn almost any shape into a tiling pattern. Finally, we develop the tessellation idea a step further, to produce more complex patterns.

Tessellation is a mathematical technique that lends itself very well to tiling. Many tiling patterns are in fact tessellations. A tessellated pattern is one in which a shape is repeated and fitted together perfectly, like a jigsaw puzzle, leaving no gaps.

Squares, isosceles and equilateral triangles, rectangles, parallelograms, regular hexagons and trapeziums all tessellate easily. A classic tessellation in nature is the honeycomb from a beehive, which is a tessellation of regular hexagons – which cannot be reproduced on a square grid. Some shapes, such as regular octagons, will not tessellate perfectly by themselves but will do so if you add another shape, such as a square, into the pattern.

To check whether a shape will tessellate, cut it out and draw around it, then move it to see if it can fit next to itself without gaps. Repeat this process, perhaps using some kind of symmetrical method, to see if the whole space can be filled. Tessellation can be an addictive pastime!

Tessellation for tiling

Let us now look at tessellation specifically for tiling purposes.

Everyone is familiar with the simple pattern of laying square tiles in two colors: the "checkerboard" pattern. The checkerboard pattern is in fact a tessellation of squares.

Although the checkerboard pattern is well known, it is still an undeniably powerful pattern, in which contrast and positive and negative shapes attract the eyes. For example, in a classic checkerboard pattern, first the white squares with black spaces are visualized, then the black squares with white spaces are visualized.

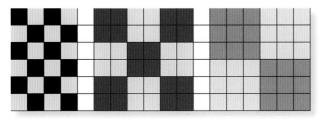

3.1 Three Different Square Checkerboard Patterns

The patterns here show simple checkerboard tessellated squares.

It can be difficult to think of workable variations on the checkerboard pattern. There can be limitations due to a lack of knowledge of the possibilities and a lack of understanding of the techniques for making tessellated patterns on a square grid. Some examples of such possibilities and techniques follow.

Many tiling patterns involving two or three colors are actually an elaboration of the well-known checkerboard style. Many patterns involve tessellations of one or more shapes. The simplest tessellation is the square, as we have seen in the previous checkerboard examples. Square tessellations can be made up of one, four, nine, or 16 squares, and so on. Rectangles are similar.

Simple variations on these shapes can produce more interesting patterns, for example triangles, parallelograms, diamonds or arrowheads. Drawing 3.2 shows a number of such examples.

3.2 Tessellated Triangles, Diamonds, Parallelograms and Bricks

Tessellations of one shape

To produce patterns of varied shapes that still fit together in a checkerboard style, the basic mathematical techniques of tessellation need to be understood.

A new shape that will tessellate is created by modifying a shape that already tessellates, for example, any of the shapes on the previous page or any sized square or rectangle.

To modify the shape correctly, "push in" an indentation on one side of the shape and "push out" an identical piece on the opposite side of the shape. This ensures that the shape will fit together and tessellate perfectly.

For example, an arrowhead can be created by pushing in a triangle at the bottom edge of a square and pushing out an identical triangle at the top edge:

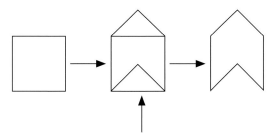

When creating a shape for tessellation, it is a good idea to draw the shape on squared paper, then cut it out, duplicate it and try to fit the pieces together like a jigsaw puzzle.

When putting color into the new design, it sometimes becomes necessary to use three colors rather than two. This is because the side edge of the new shape may touch more than one other shape when the pieces are fitted together.

The following pages have some examples of these creative tessellations. Note how the left-hand side of each drawing shows the original shape from which the new design has been derived.

3.3 Arrowheads

This pattern demonstrates the creative tessellation process quite clearly. The tops and bottoms of the squares have been pushed up, creating an arrowhead design that still resembles the original checkerboard in some way.

3.4 Corners

Here we have altered parallelograms, pushing out (and pushing in) a corner. This produces a shifting design quite different from the original, which needs three colors to display it clearly.

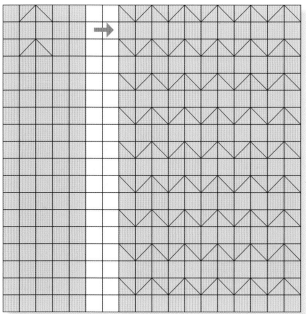

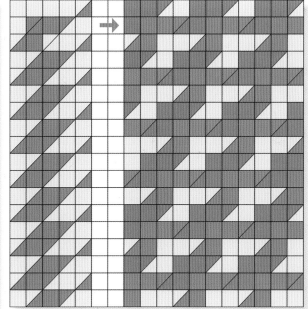

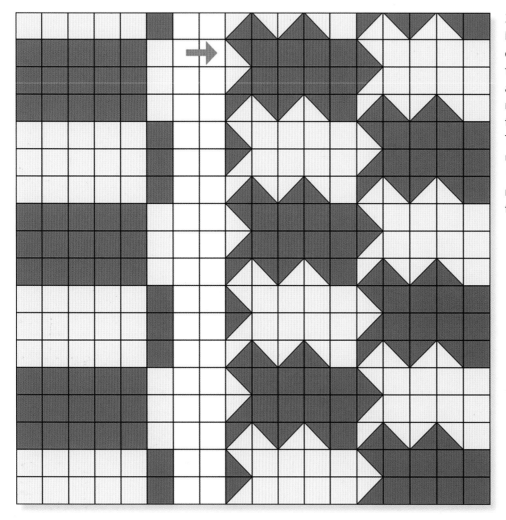

3.5 Animals

Here we have pushed out three triangles from a long rectangle and pushed in three matching triangles on the opposite sides. This produces the unusual complex "animal" shape that, nevertheless, still fits together perfectly.

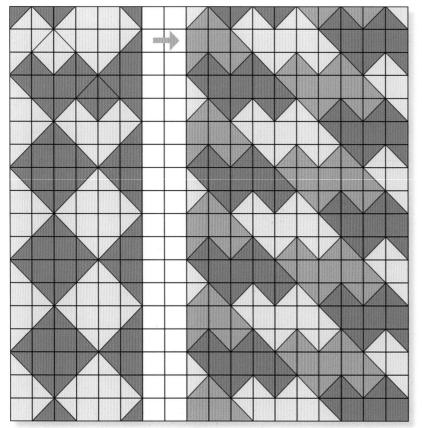

3.6 Cobblestones (1)

Here a diamond has been altered by pushing out (and pushing in) a square. This produces a cobblestone shape that we often see in real paving stones for driveways and footpaths.

Here are a few more tessellated tile designs made with one shape:

3.7 Bricks – Two Alternatives

This is a common herringbone design usually seen when bricks are laid as paving stones, as seen in the photo on the right. Two alternatives are shown: one with the bricks lying horizontally or vertically (top), and one with them lying diagonally (above). Notice the completely different effects.

Repeating unit (for diagonal pattern): 6 x 4.

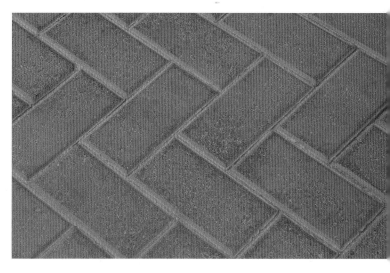

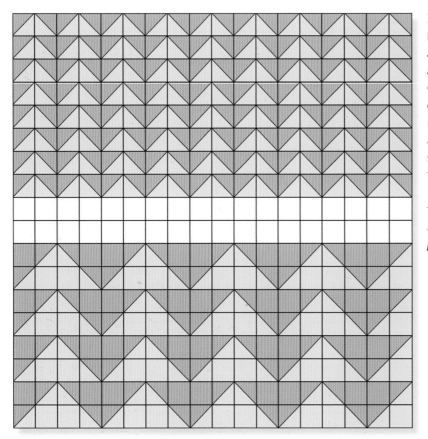

3.8 Triangle Experiment (1)

Here two sizes of repeated triangles are shown, illustrating how different a design can look if its size is altered. Comparing this to the triangles in drawing 3.2, we see that they are now placed directly beneath one another, and the coloring choice suggests a row of hills or coniferous trees. (See also drawings 10.51 and 10.52 for simple border versions of these triangles.)

Repeating unit (larger pattern): 4 x 2.

3.9 Triangle Experiment (2)

Playing with exactly the same design as in drawing 3.8, we see that coloring it differently highlights a zigzag pattern. Once again, size variation is a significant factor in the final effect.
(See also drawings 10.53 and 10.54 for these patterns treated as borders.)

Repeating unit (large zigzag): 4 x 4.

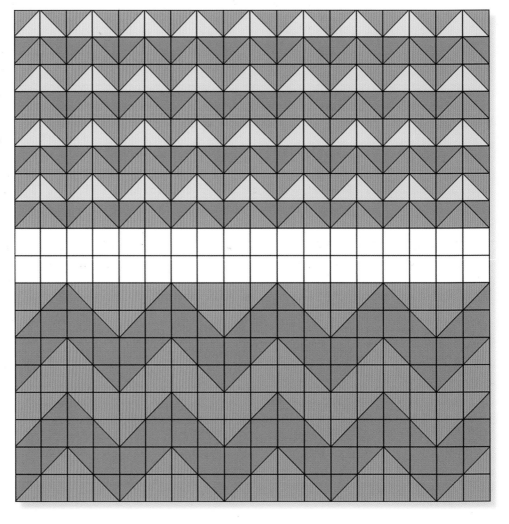

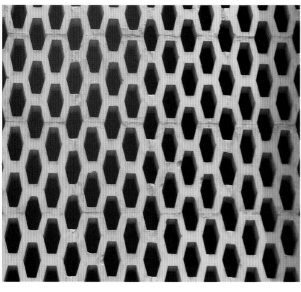

3.10 Hexagons

This is as close as we can get with square tiles to the honeycomb pattern produced in beehives. The shape is not true to nature since it is not a regular hexagon. When we compare this drawing with the window grille in the photo on the left, we find that it is essentially the same pattern rotated 90 degrees and stretched. (See also drawing 10.55, in which the pattern is used as a border, producing the look of a row of flowers.)
Repeating unit: 6 x 4.

3.11 Cobblestones (2)

This is another common shape used in concrete paving stones, as shown in the photo on the left.
Repeating unit: 8 x 8.

3.12 Falling Leaves

This is a common wall and window grille decoration in the Middle East. It is usually shown as a slimmer shape. For example, in the photo above (from a mosque in Dubai, U.A.E.), the leaf is slimmer, facing upward and has some rounded lines. (See drawing 10.59 for this pattern treated as a border.)
Repeating unit: 8 x 8.

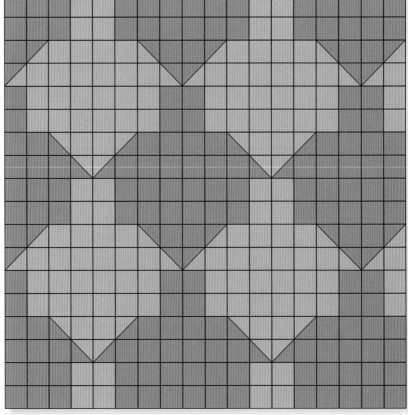

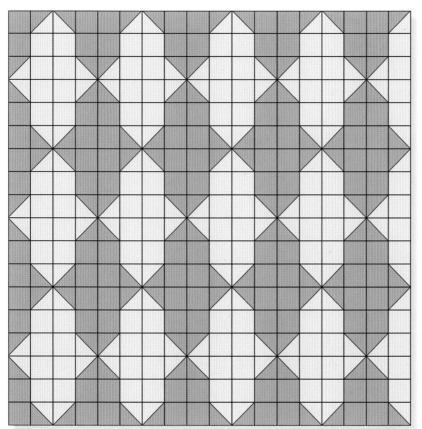

3.13 Medina Motif

This elegant design is often used in metal grilles in the Middle East. This one is based on a fence at the Prophet's Mosque, Medina, Saudi Arabia, as shown in the photo above. (See drawing 10.56 for this pattern treated as a border.)
Repeating unit: 4 x 6.

3.14 Fading Diamonds

Although this is not strictly a tessellation of one shape, it is included here to illustrate another possibility: varying the size of tessellated shapes to produce interesting effects. In this drawing there is a pleasant illusion of the diamonds fading away into the distance. It is based on the wooden window grille shown in the photo above left (from Satwa, Dubai, U.A.E.).

Finally in this chapter we will examine more of the tessellated artworks of M.C. Escher and attempt to render them into tiling patterns. Those who are familiar with the artist's work will recognize the designs, some of which were inspired by decorative work at the Alhambra in Spain.

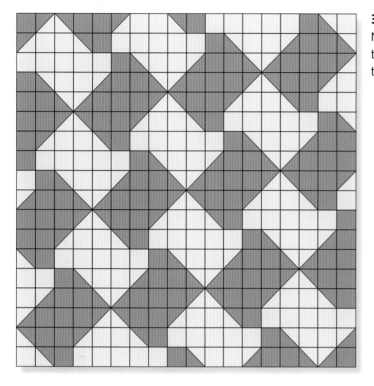

3.15 Flounder (Flatfish)
Note how this design achieves a successful tessellation by turning the shape by 90 degrees to make it fit.

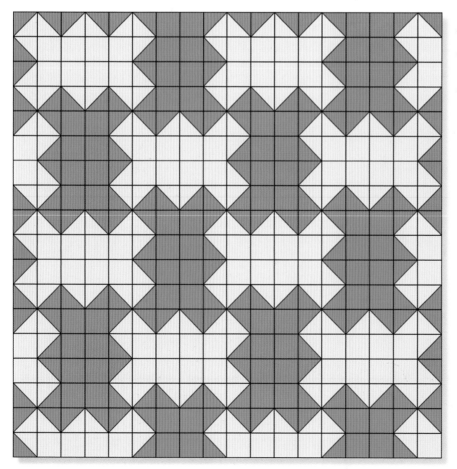

3.16 Cobblestones (3)
This design is found on decorative work in mosques in both Iran and Turkey.
Repeating unit: 8 x 8.

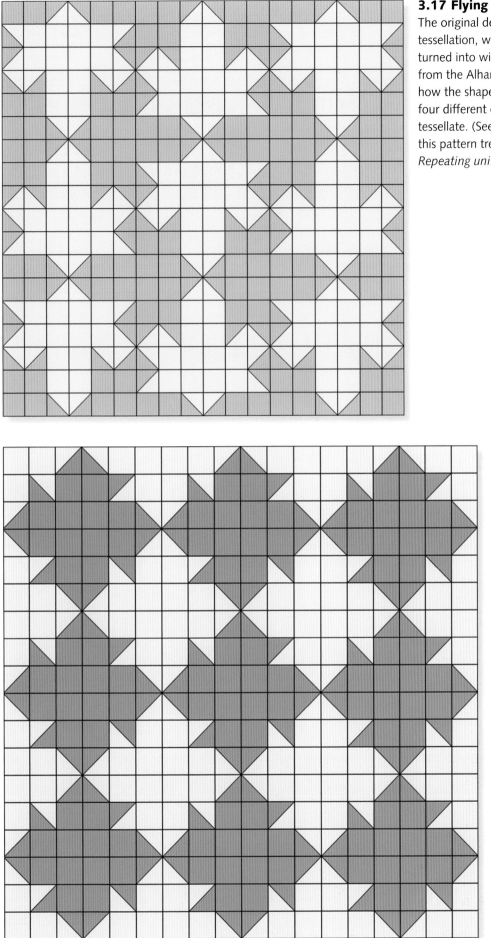

3.17 Flying Insects

The original design of this tessellation, which M.C. Escher turned into winged creatures, came from the Alhambra in Spain. Note how the shape has been turned in four different directions to make it tessellate. (See drawing 10.58 for this pattern treated as a border.) *Repeating unit: 12 x 12.*

3.18 Flying Fish

Repeating unit: 6 x 6.

3.19 Horsemen

This design is fun because of the way the horsemen alternately walk in opposite directions. (See drawing 10.57 for this pattern treated as a border.)
Repeating unit: 4 x 4.

3.20 Interlocking Bars

This is a classic and very old Islamic design that has become popular in modern times as a metal fence or gate grille, as shown above (from Satwa, Dubai, U.A.E.).

Chapter 4

TESSELLATIONS OF TWO SHAPES

When working with a shape for tessellation, sometimes we can modify it in an "imperfect" way, by not following the method described in chapter 3 precisely. Doing this often produces two or more shapes that can work together in a design that appears even more fascinating and complex.

The following pages show tiling patterns that are examples of two tessellated shapes.

4.1 Diagonal Cross

To create a pleasing, balanced design, success can often be achieved by choosing shapes that have one or two axes of reflective symmetry, or that have rotational symmetry through half or quarter turns.

For example, in the drawing at right, both shapes have four axes of reflective symmetry meaning that we could draw four different "mirror lines" through the shape that would make it look as if half of it reflects perfectly onto the other half. The mirror lines would lie vertically, horizontally and on both diagonals. This means that the shape is highly symmetrical.

Each shape also has what is termed "rotational symmetry of order four," which means that if we rotated the shape around its center, it would map onto itself exactly after turning through 90, 180, 270 and 360 degrees. Again this means that the shape is highly symmetrical in a rotational sense.

The drawing is based on the plaster wall decoration shown in the photo above left (from Dubai, U.A.E.).
Repeating unit: 8 x 4.

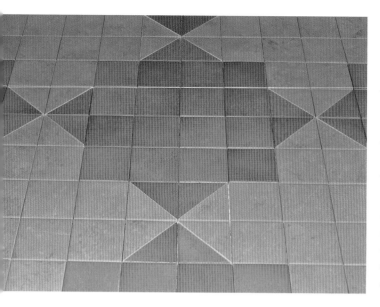

4.2 Iranian Checkerboard

Comparing drawings 4.1 and 4.2, we can see that while one shape is identical in each design, the other is different. This is because of positioning. In drawing 4.1 the rotated squares (or eight-pointed stars) are placed in diagonal rows, while in drawing 4.2 they are lined up vertically and horizontally. This is a good example of how the placing of shapes in a design can give a completely different result. (See also drawing 10.65 for this design treated as a border.)

Both drawings 4.1 and 4.2 are popular in modern Middle Eastern grilles and surface decorations. The design in drawing 4.2 was originally found on the walls of mosques in Iran. The photo on the left shows tiles laid out according to the design in drawing 4.2.

Repeating unit: 6 x 6.

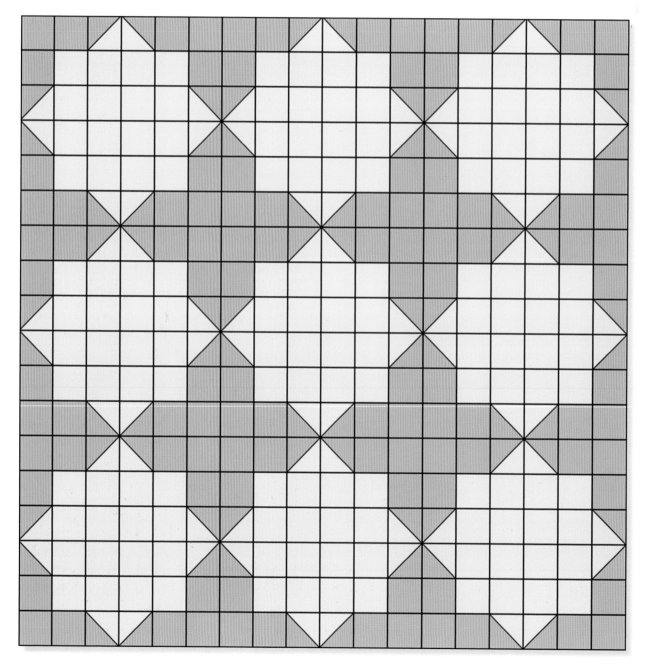

4.3 Taj Stars

This design is one of the many beautiful surface decorations on the Taj Mahal in India. The basis of the pattern is a long hexagon placed alternately lying down and standing up. The four-pointed stars then appear in the spaces, seeming to dance from side to side as we move our eyes across the pattern. (See drawing 10.67 for this design treated as a border.)

Repeating unit: 6 x 6.

4.4 Marching Hexagons

A different arrangement of smaller hexagons produces a much more regimented design, this time with diamonds

filling the spaces. It is a surprisingly effective pattern when used as an open grille on fences, as shown in the photo below of a wooden fence (from Dubai, U.A.E.). A patterned fence grille teamed with the same design on a tiled patio could look very good. (See drawing 10.44 for this pattern treated as a border.)

Repeating unit: 2 x 3.

4.5 Marching Octagons

This time an octagon was chosen as a base shape and again placed regimentally in rows, creating diamonds in the spaces. An octagon will only "tessellate" if a square or diamond is added in, as shown here. It is a popular design for concrete grilles in the Middle East, as well as for interesting paving designs, as shown in the grille and path photos at the bottom (from Dubai, U.A.E.).

Repeating unit: 3 x 3.

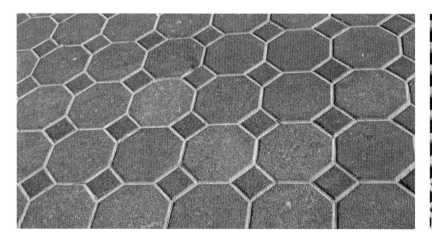

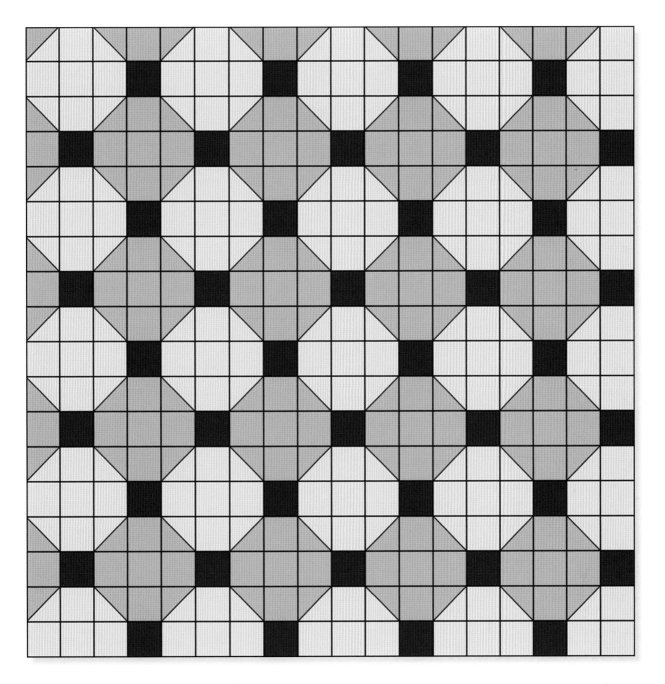

4.6 Octagon Checkerboard

Drawings 4.5 and 4.6 differ only in placement of the octagons. Here the octagons are lined up diagonally, so that a square appears in the spaces. An unusual tiled wall in this design is shown in the photo on the left (from Dubai, U.A.E.). The tiles were made in small square and quarter octagon shapes and put together in mosaic fashion.

Repeating unit: 4 x 4.

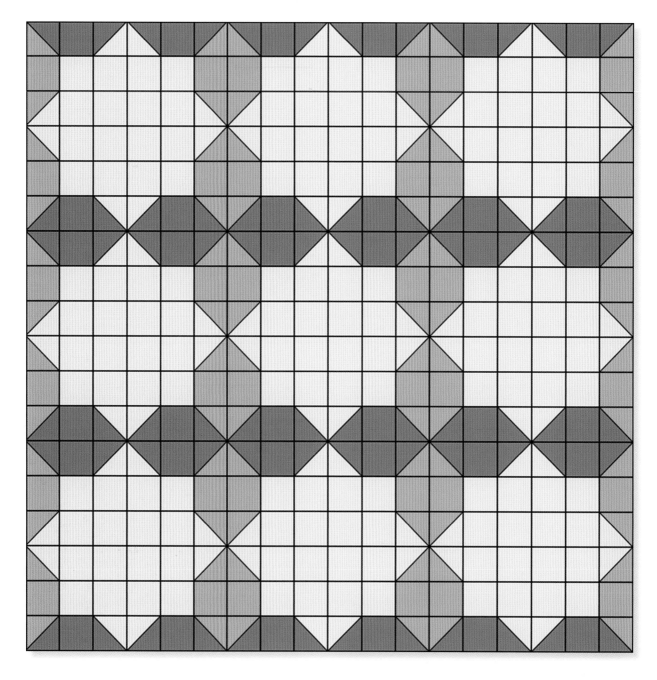

4.7 Star Grille

Drawings 4.7 and 4.2 are very similar. Here the vertical cross has been divided up to make four hexagons, resulting in an emphasis on the horizontal and vertical components of the pattern. The design is well suited to use as a metal grille and is often utilized in this way. The photo on the right shows a rather beautiful way to decorate something functional: a heavy sliding gate for a driveway (from Dubai, U.A.E.). It is easy to imagine the impact that could be obtained from opening the gate and seeing the same pattern repeated on a tiled courtyard or wall inside. (See also drawing 10.64 for this pattern treated as a border.)
Repeating unit: 6 x 6.

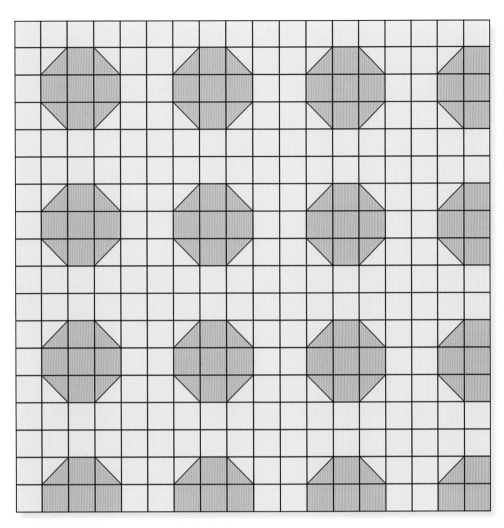

4.8 Octagon Windows

This is a very simple, open design, similar to one seen often in tiling, except that a diamond is usually used for visual interest. *Repeating unit: 5 x 5.*

4.9 Square Windows

This is another simple tiling design, often echoed in concrete block walls. *Repeating unit: 4 x 4.*

4.10 Syrian Stars

Compare the design above with drawings 4.3 and 4.5. Here the offset placement of octagons has made four-pointed stars appear to drift gently downward as the eye follows the pattern.
Repeating unit: 10 x 10.

4.11 Star Flowers

This fun design is the only way to produce six-pointed stars with square tiles. Each star is surrounded by a rosette of hexagons that, when viewed from a distance, looks like petals on a flower.
Repeating unit: 4 x 4.

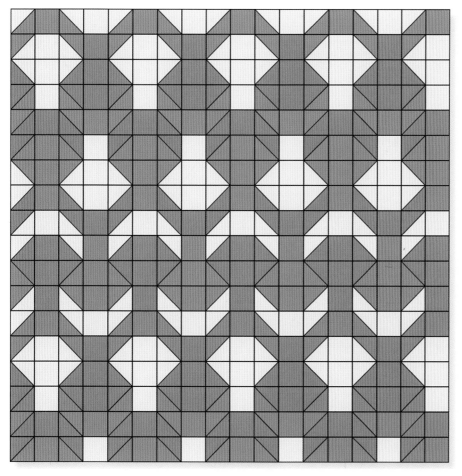

4.12 Hexagon Hills

This is a remarkably rounded-looking design, not often achieved when working with tiles. We imagine we can see rolling hills, and we get a sense of infinity. The pattern requires a fairly complex coloring scheme, so that even though the shapes are the same in each row, the colors do not repeat until the fourth row. (See also drawing 10.42 for this pattern treated as a border.)
Repeating unit: 4 x 12.

4.13 Octagons and Cotton Spools

This design is an interesting study in positives and negatives. The octagons and "cotton spools" are alternately colored dark and light, so that we see first one as real and the other as a background, then vice versa.
Repeating unit: 8 x 8.

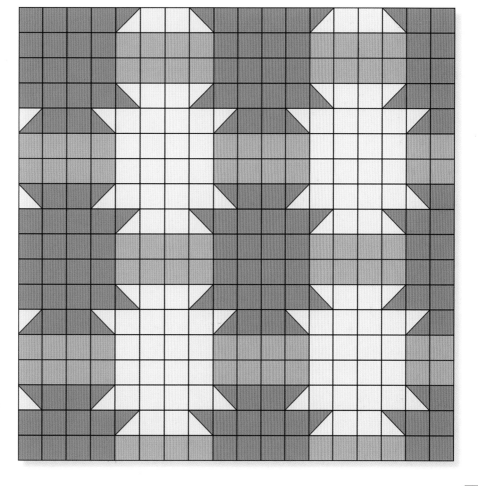

4.14 Coffee Pot Grid

This design came about by altering drawing 4.13 and scaling it down. The "coffee pots" emerged when trying to create a shape that would tessellate.

Repeating unit: 5 x 5.

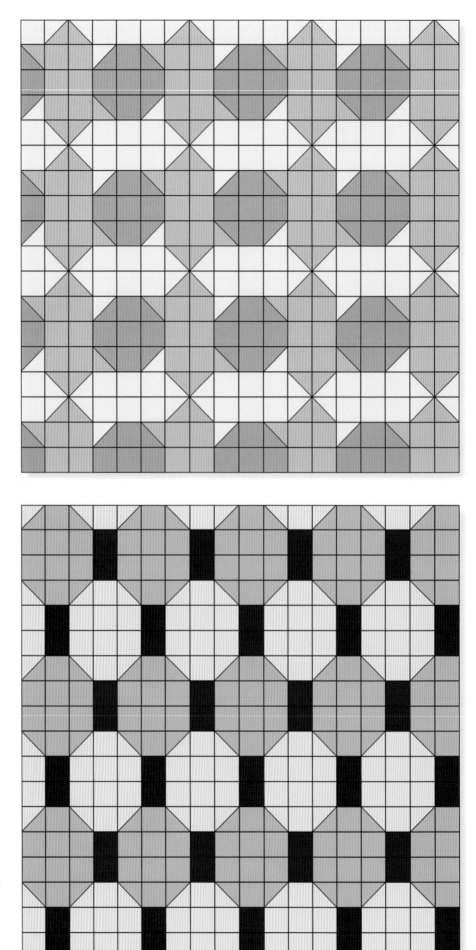

4.15 Octagon Grille

This simple design, like drawing 4.12, manages to achieve a rounded look. It is a useful design for concrete block grilles, and therefore it could be effective as a patio tile design when teamed up with such a wall.

Repeating unit: 4 x 6.

4.16 Pinwheels

A very delicate design, this was created by altering a diamond tessellation in an "imperfect" way. (See drawing 10.45 for this pattern treated as a border.)
Repeating unit: 4 x 4.

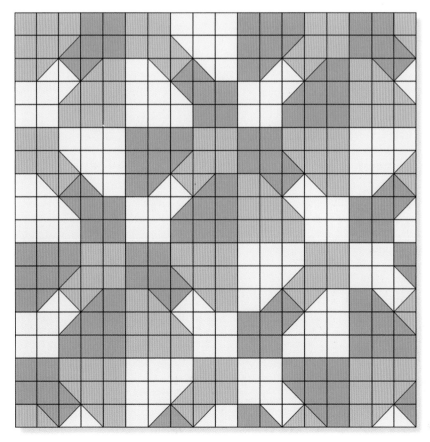

4.17 Arrow Formation

This interesting design is based on a square with arrows on opposite diagonals. As the square rotates, we get a "crazy arrow" formation. The color scheme has to be quite complex in order to show the shapes. The design was found on a concrete block wall frieze and makes an interesting border pattern (see drawing 10.36).
Repeating unit: 30 x 30.

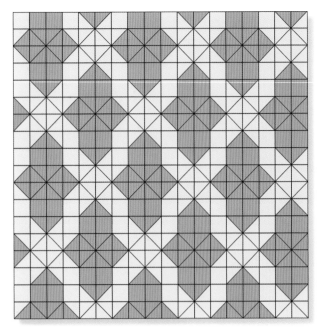

4.18 Middle Eastern Weave

This design manages to convey a very Middle Eastern flavor and has a pleasant wobbly, woven look, as if the lighter strips are weaving around the darker spaces. It was created by altering drawing 3.13, changing the thin edge of each line into a solid shape. The design could also become a border if a strip is extracted, and a real version of this can be seen as a wall tile frieze in the Imam Sadeq Grand Mosque in Bahrain. (See drawing 10.4 for this pattern treated as a border.)
Repeating unit: 6 x 8.

4.19 Moroccan Maze

This is a classic Moroccan tessellation pattern. We feel that there are more than just two shapes working together here because of the clever interaction of positive and negative colors.
Repeating unit: 16 x 16.

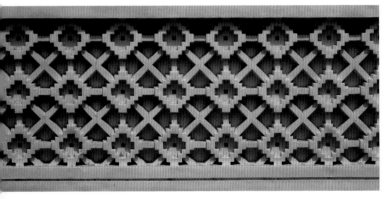

4.20 Octagon Quarters Checkerboard

This drawing simplifies the plasterwork shown in the photo above (from Dubai, U.A.E.), producing just the diamond and quarter octagon shapes. For the more complex version see drawing 6.22. In order to highlight the two shapes here, we need to use a checkerboard-style color scheme. (See also drawing 10.48 for this pattern treated as a border.)
Repeating unit: 12 x 12.

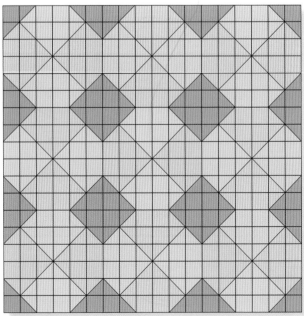

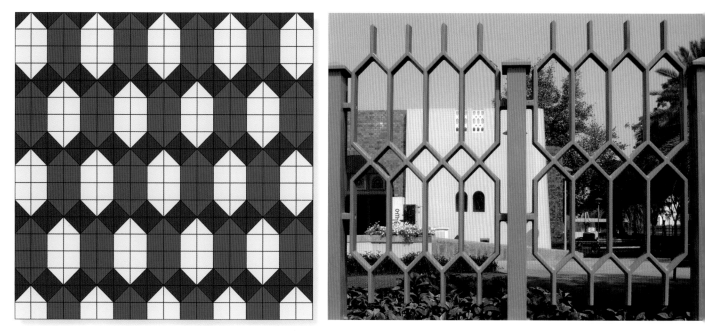

4.21 Hexagon and Diamond Checkerboard

Compare this design to drawing 4.4. Elongating the hexagons, as well as highlighting them using color, changes the effect. The inspiration here was the grille fence shown in the photo above right (from Satwa, Dubai, U.A.E.), and, as noted in other examples, a matching fence and paved courtyard could look pleasantly unified. (See drawing 10.49 for this pattern treated as a border.)

Repeating unit: 4 x 8.

4.22 Triangle Arches

Inspired by the concrete wall pictured below right (from Deira, Dubai, U.A.E.), square tiles become quite a striking pattern with interlocking triangular arches.

Repeating unit: 16 x 4.

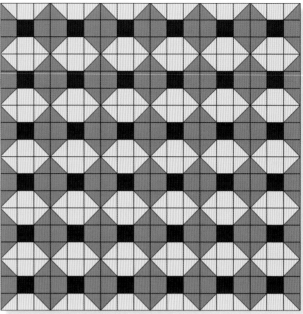

4.23 Hexagon and Square Checkerboard

Seen on the mosque windows in the photo above (from Deira, Dubai, U.A.E.), this is a simple design based on hexagons and squares.
Repeating unit: 3 x 3.

4.24 Zigzagging Hexagons

For completeness, another hexagon formation is shown here, this time with a zigzag running through it. Compare this with drawing 4.4. We can see that the difference is the offset placement of the hexagon rows, which creates the zigzag.
Repeating unit: 2 x 6.

4.25 Hexagon Parade

An interesting variation on drawing 4.24 arises when we color it differently, highlighting each shape. We suddenly arrive at a complex, woven look. (See drawing 10.50 for this pattern treated as a border.) The photo on the left shows the pattern displayed in floor tiles.
Repeating unit: 6 x 6.

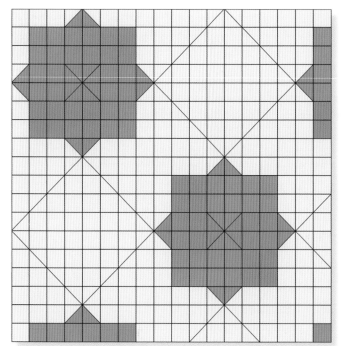

4.26 Hammerhead Checkerboard

This design uses a formation of four "hammerheads" and inserts it into a large, diagonal checkerboard. Although not strictly a two-shape tessellation, it is included here for interest and because of its close relationship with the drawing that follows.
Repeating unit: 16 x 16.

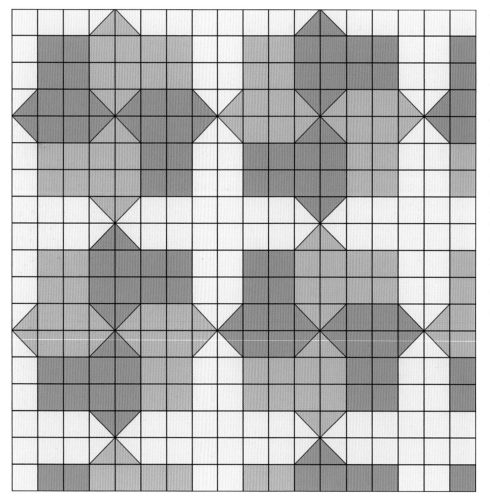

4.27 Hammerhead Formations

Compare this design with drawing 4.2. Here the eight-pointed star has been divided into four "hammerhead" shapes that rotate around a center, as in drawing 4.26. We almost imagine a swirling effect of little whirlpools when we view the pattern from a distance. (See drawing 10.47 for this pattern treated as a border.)
Repeating unit: 8 x 8.

We have seen in the last two chapters that one- and two-shape tessellations can make highly successful tile patterns. Tiles are a fun way to experiment with these designs, with the possibilities being literally endless!

Chapter 5

Tessellations of three shapes

As the numbers of shapes that are fitted together increases, so does the complexity of the design. However, it is interesting to note that the minimum number of colors required to clearly display the pattern often remains at two or, at most, three. This is a bonus for the application of floor tiling because it is not always desirable to have too many colors on a tiled surface.

Below are a number of designs that are made up of three tessellated shapes. As always, these merely represent a starting point from which many more patterns can be created.

5.1 Falling Squares
This drawing is a classic Middle Eastern design, reproduced in the tile pattern in the photo above. The squares are of differing sizes and are placed at different angles, all working together to produce an illusion of movement. We think we see endless cubes tumbling downward. The design is also often used as a frieze, looking quite different to what we see here. (See drawing 10.40 for this pattern treated as a border.)

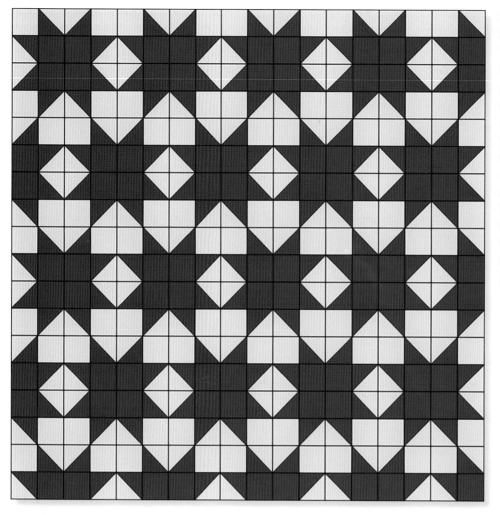

5.2 Regimented Stars

This drawing shows classic eight-pointed stars in slightly offset rows, creating diamond- and pentagon-shaped spaces. This is a basic design from which many complex Middle Eastern patterns stem. (See drawing 10.41 for this pattern treated as a border.)
Repeating unit: 4 x 8.

5.3 Diamond Windows

Compare this with drawing 4.2. It is not easy to notice that this is the same drawing with a diamond inserted into each shape, creating an illusion of looking through a complex series of windows.
Repeating unit: 6 x 6.

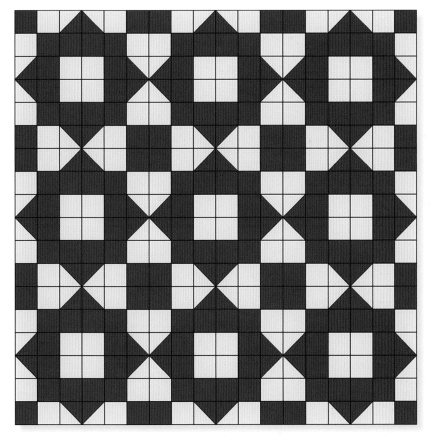

5.4 Square Windows

Here the same pattern as in drawing 4.2 has had squares inserted into the spaces. Note also how a change of colors can have a great affect on the look of the pattern.

Repeating unit: 6 x 6.

5.5 Taj Mahal Splendor

This drawing takes the design of drawing 4.1 and inserts diamonds inside the shapes.
The result is a much more complex-looking pattern that graces the walls of the Taj Mahal in India.

Repeating unit: 8 x 8.

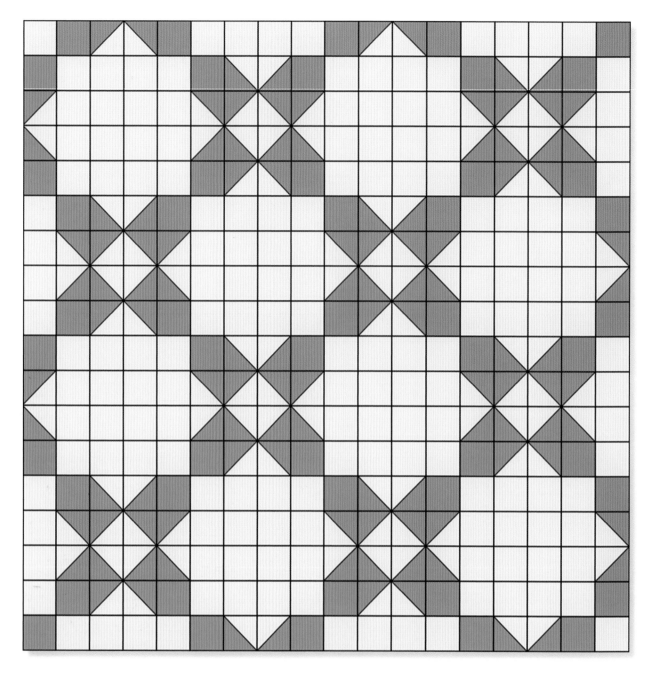

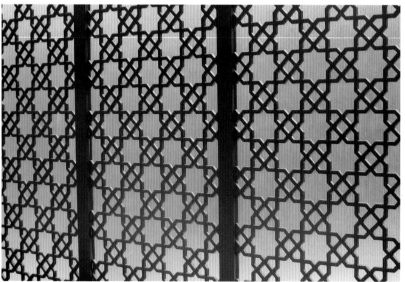

5.6 Diagonal Grille

This design is a simplified version of drawing 5.5, with one of the squares removed. It is a very popular design for modern grille work in the Middle East, as shown in the photo on the left (from Dubai, U.A.E.). Once again, having the same design on, say, a gate as well as on a paved courtyard or wall could be very effective.
Repeating unit: 8 x 8.

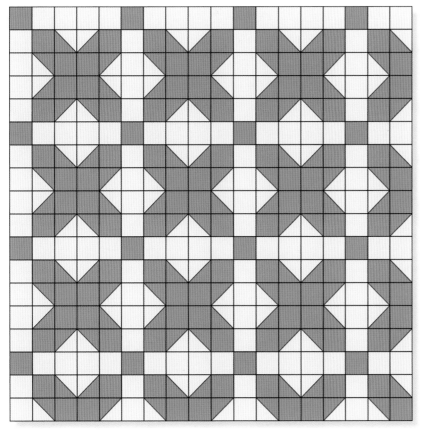

5.7 Afghan Cross

Another classic design found in mosques in Afghanistan and Iran. It is often echoed in today's modern architectural decorations.
Repeating unit: 5 x 5.

5.8 Concrete Block

This simple design is a matching tile version of a commonly used concrete block, as seen in the photo of the wall below right. If the design was seen both in a wall and on a tiled floor, it would give a unified effect.
Repeating unit: 9 x 9.

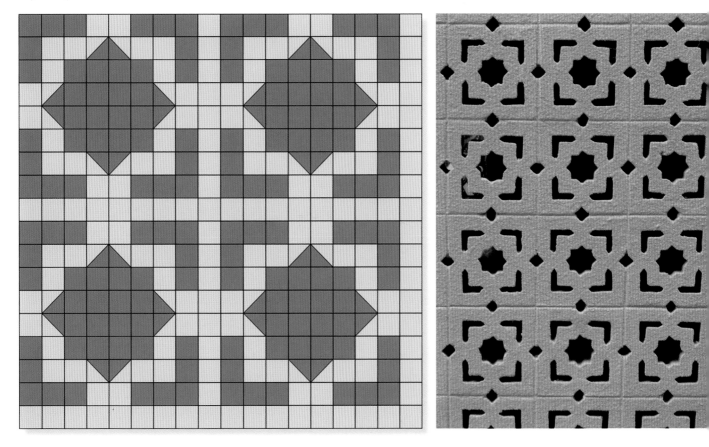

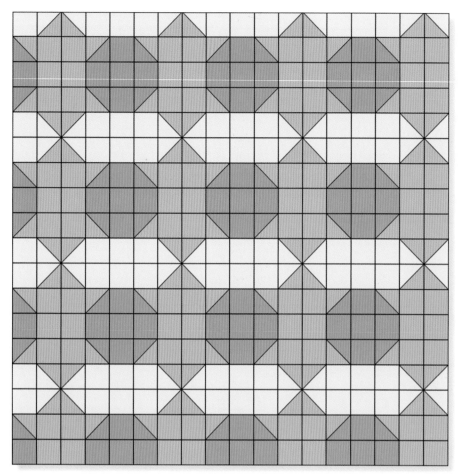

5.9 Cotton Spool Rows

This design has taken drawing 4.14 and altered it slightly, producing a row of long hexagons and a more regimented pattern. (See drawing 10.43 for this pattern treated as a border.)
Repeating unit: 5 x 5.

5.10 Dripping Diamonds

This is a simple and very different design from what we have been focusing on. It could look striking or subtle, depending on the choice of colors. (See drawing 10.6 for this pattern treated as a border.)
Repeating unit: 8 x 8.

5.11 Mixed Checkerboard

Compare this design to drawing 4.18. It is the same design but colored so that different shapes are highlighted, particularly the rows of diamonds. The effect is like a checkerboard of four-, five- and six-sided shapes. (See drawing 10.5 for this pattern treated as a border.)
Repeating unit: 6 x 8.

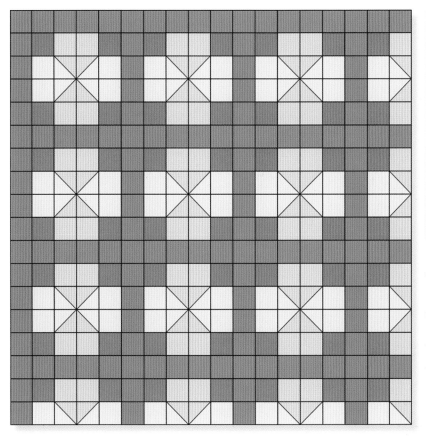

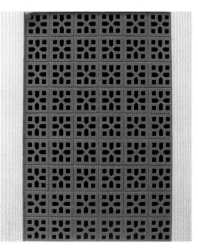

5.12 Square Grid Block

This is a tile version of a commonly used concrete block design, as shown in the photo above (from Dubai, U.A.E.). (See drawing 10.37 for this pattern treated as a border.)
Repeating unit: 5 x 5.

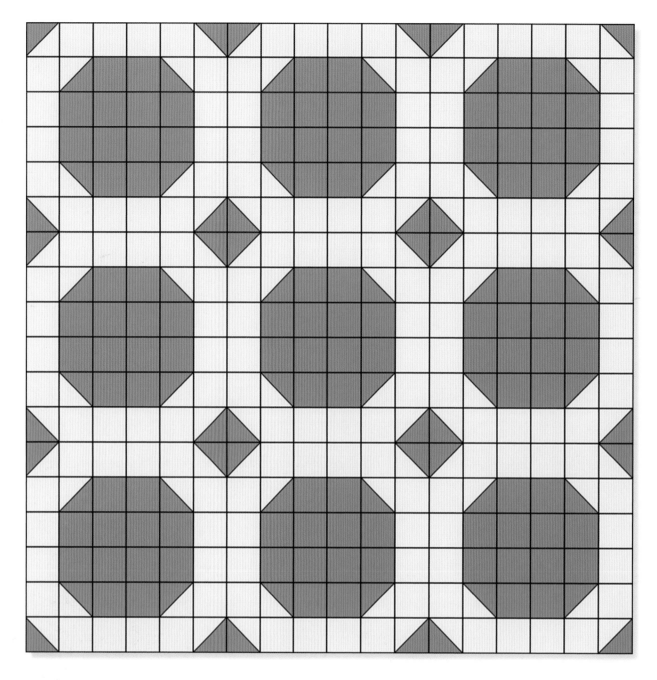

5.13 Octagon Grid Block

Again, we have a common concrete block pattern, shown in the photo (from Dubai, U.A.E.), rendered as a simple tile design.

Repeating unit: 6 x 6.

5.14 Diamond and Hexagon Grille

This is the tile version of the pattern seen in the photo of a metal grille fence, below right (from Dubai, U.A.E.).

Repeating unit: 4 x 8.

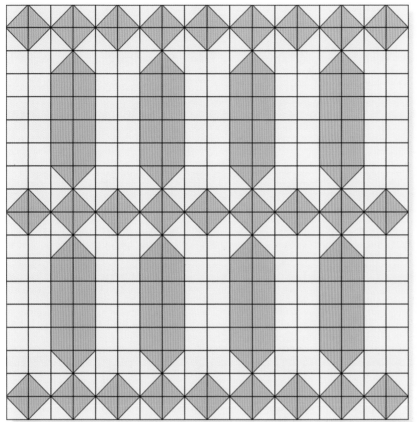

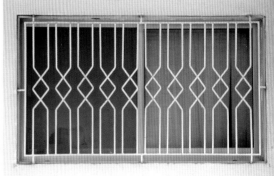

5.15 Diamond and Hexagon Bars

This is the tile version of the pattern seen on metal window bars in the photo above (from Dubai, U.A.E.).

Repeating unit: 3 x 8.

5.16 Qusais Diamonds

This elegant design once more renders a common modern Middle Eastern grille pattern into tiles.
Repeating unit: 12 x 12.

5.17 Brunei Brilliance

This clever design is very pleasing to the eye. It is used throughout the famous Jame Asr Hassanil Bolkiah Mosque in Brunei, on walls and windows, in an interesting variety of ways. (See drawing 10.46 for this pattern treated as a border.)
Repeating unit: 12 x 12.

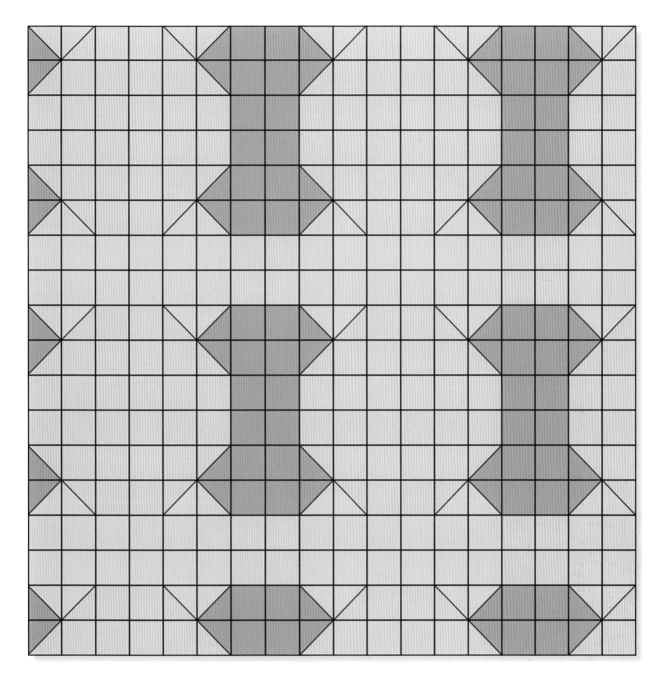

5.18 Complex Cobblestones

Here is another design inspired by footpath cobblestones, as shown in the photo on the left (from Dubai, U.A.E.). It is nice to have a tiling alternative to these cobblestone patterns because the stones themselves are not always readily available.

Repeating unit: 8 x 8.

5.19 Egyptian Diamonds

This pattern was inspired by a concrete wall found in Egypt. *Repeating unit: 14 x 14.*

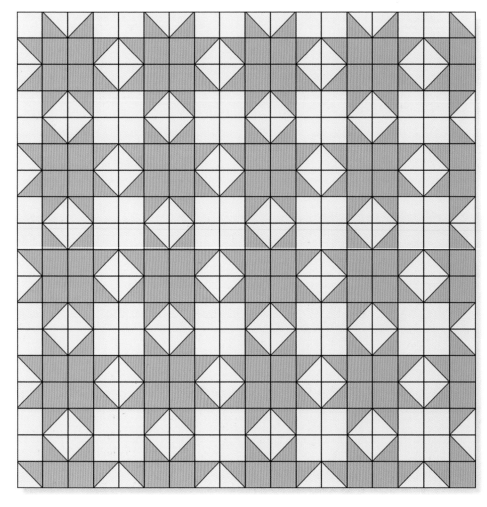

5.20 Straight Star Checkerboard

Compare this design to drawing 5.2. Here the small eight-pointed stars are lined up horizontally and vertically, creating squares and diamonds in the spaces. The regimental alignment reminds us of a conventional checkerboard. *Repeating unit: 4 x 4.*

5.21 Diagonal Star Checkerboard

Once again we have the illusion of a checkerboard, with the same small eight-pointed stars this time lined up diagonally.
Repeating unit: 6 x 6.

5.22 Drifting Star Grid

In a final different alignment of the same small eight-pointed star, the shifted positions make it appear as if rows of stars are drifting sideways and downward.
Repeating unit: 15 x 15.

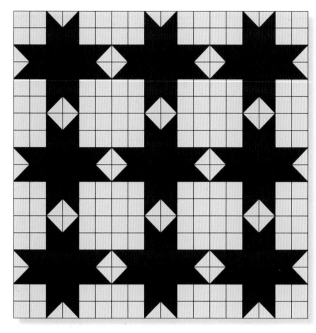

5.23 Tall Star Vertical Grid

Here we see a taller eight-pointed star lined up horizontally and vertically. The result is a much more regimented look than drawing 5.20.
Repeating unit: 6 x 6.

5.24 Tall Star Diagonal Grid

This time the taller stars are lined up diagonally, yet we still get a straight checkerboard effect.
Repeating unit: 8 x 8.

5.25 Middle Eastern Checkerboard

This is actually the same design as drawing 4.18, but it is colored so that the small eight-pointed star is highlighted.
Repeating unit: 6 x 8.

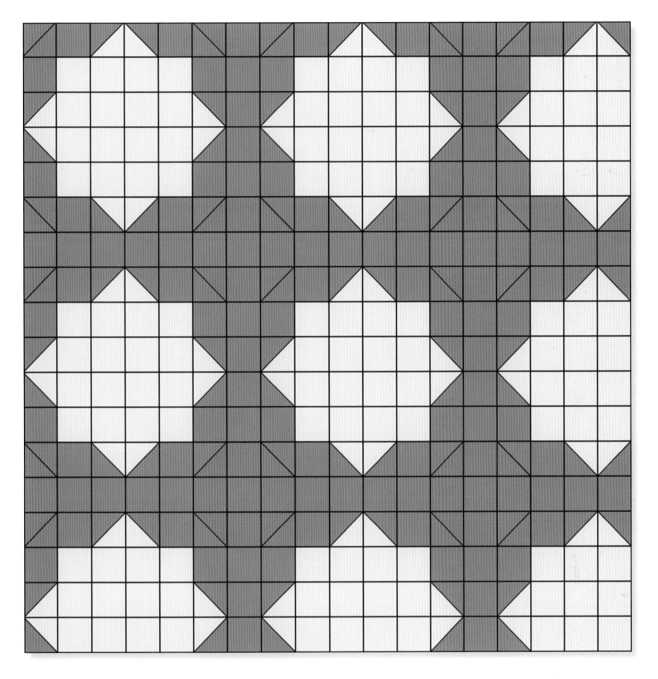

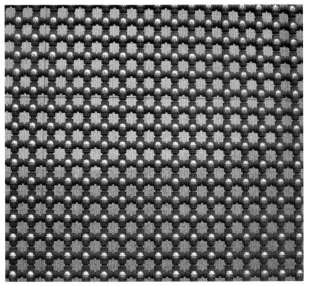

5.26 Brunei Grid

This is a tile rendering of a design found on a wooden screen in the Hassanil Bolkiah Mosque in Brunei, shown in the photo on the left.

Repeating unit: 7 x 7.

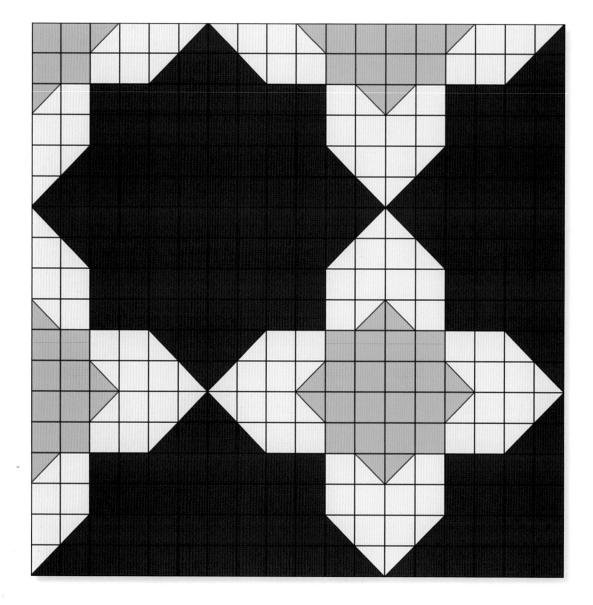

5.27 Brunei Courtyard

This design was inspired by the dramatic tiled courtyard of the Jame Asr Hassanil Bolkiah Mosque in Brunei. The pattern has been simplified and shrunk slightly to be more applicable to smaller spaces. Notice in the photo that the method of tiling is in a mosaic style, which is difficult to achieve if you are unskilled in the art of mosaic making. This drawing shows a way to reproduce a very similar effect using a square tile grid.
Repeating unit: 12 x 12.

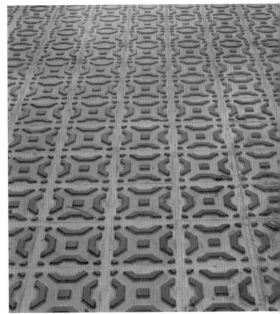

5.28 Deira Driveway

Inspired by a driveway surface, this is a simple three-shape checkerboard style design. It is similar but subtly different from drawing 5.13. For a more complex version that looks more like the driveway in the photo (from Deira, Dubai, U.A.E.), see drawing 6.5.

5.29 Concrete Block Maze

Compare this design with drawing 5.12 and its accompanying photo. The "edges" of the blocks have been removed, and the resulting pattern reveals a square within an octagon, with the whole effect looking like a maze.
Repeating unit: 9 x 9.

5.30 Lamps

This design has a definite "kitcheny" feel and would be best suited to small wall tiles. (See drawing 10.19 for this pattern as a border.)
Repeating unit: 8 x 5.

5.31 Dancing Star Maze

This is a fun design with rows of dancing stars embedded within hexagons and octagons.

Chapter 6

More complex tessellations

Of course, we can go on creating tessellation patterns that have yet more shapes and appear increasingly more complex. Often these more complex patterns are produced by breaking up a simple tessellation, by adding more lines. All these patterns have symmetry and the potential for infinite repetition in all directions, making each one a visual feast.

Examples of tessellations using more than three shapes follow.

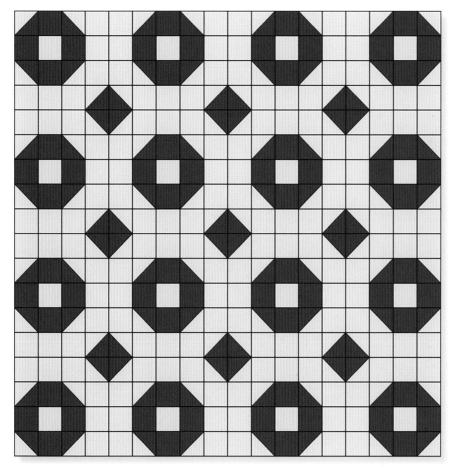

6.1 Nuts and Bolts
Although this drawing is complex because it has a number of shapes, the relative positioning of these shapes creates a very simple design.
Repeating unit: 5 x 5.

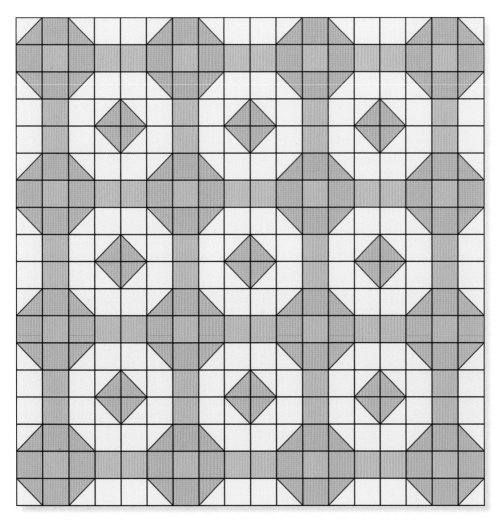

6.2 Nuts and Bolts Grid

The same design as in drawing 6.1 attains a very different feel to it when "bars" are inserted to form a grid pattern.
Repeating unit: 5 x 5.

6.3 Octagon Grid Maze

This time, with an octagon grid lined up diagonally, we get the interesting effect of positive and negative colorings required to display the pattern. (See drawing 7.36 for this design as a small motif.)
Repeating unit: 6 x 6.

6.4 Octagon Checkerboard

This design plays with the checkerboard idea, inserting octagons into it. Many shapes could be used in a similar way for a variation on simple checkerboard-style tile patterns.
Repeating unit: 8 x 8.

6.5 Deira Driveway Detail

Comparing this pattern with drawing 5.28 and its accompanying photo, we see that it is a truer rendering of the real driveway that inspired the design.
Repeating unit: 9 x 9.

6.6 Eight-Pointed Star Checkerboard

This design is fascinating because the more you look, the more you see. At first it looks like an altered checkerboard with some triangles inserted. Then the eye picks up the small eight-pointed star created by the "rotated square" shape. Finally, if we view the pattern from a distance and refocus, the large, classic eight-pointed stars appear in formation.
Repeating unit: 10 x 10.

6.7 Diamond Lattice

Now we are really exploring complex geometric tile patterns! This design has taken the much simpler design pictured in drawing 4.1 and transformed it, simply by adding a large diamond and a square into the original shapes.
Repeating unit: 8 x 8.

6.8 Snowflakes

Looking closely, we can see that this design is built with large diamonds lined up on a diagonal grid. Extra horizontal and vertical lines then break up the shapes to create smaller ones. Viewed from a distance, the grid lines all but disappear, and we see an array of starry snowflakes. This pattern could look dazzling in small tiles on a feature wall.
Repeating unit: 10 x 10.

6.9 Exploding Stars

This pattern is built from vertically aligned diamonds and zigzags, with horizontal and vertical grid lines creating new shapes. The classic eight-pointed star is a dominant feature. From a distance we imagine we see exploding stars. This design would be suitable for a feature wall where the small tiles would allow us to quickly appreciate the whole picture.
Repeating unit: 12 x 12.

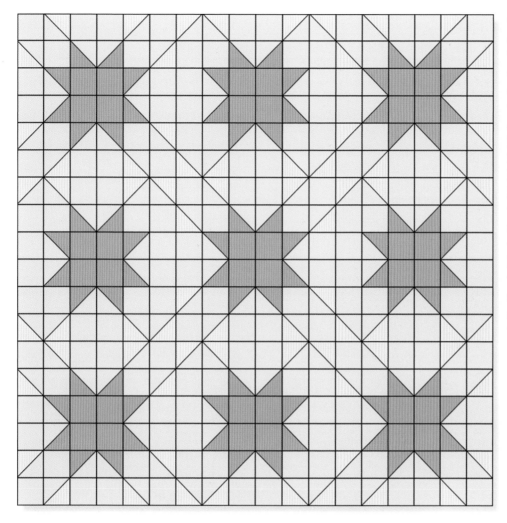

6.10 Star Lattice

A more regimented version of an array of dazzling stars, this design almost has a three-dimensional appearance. We imagine we are looking through a lattice with glimpses of light coming through from the other side. (See drawing 7.44 for a version of the hexagon star motif that is central to this design.)
Repeating unit: 12 x 12.

6.11 Snowflakes with Squares

Based once again on an array of diagonally aligned diamonds, this is another dazzling design that would be suitable for a feature wall. The inclusion of the squares has an unusual "bending" effect on the lines when we view the pattern from a distance.
Repeating unit: 8 x 8.

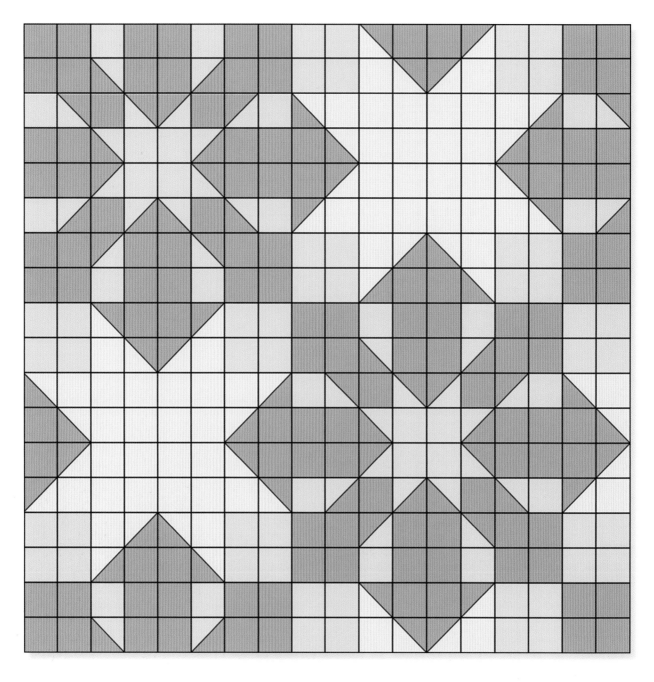

6.12 Flower Mass

This drawing incorporates two classic Middle Eastern shapes: the eight-pointed star and the arrowhead star. These are seen in endless variations in architectural decorations, both ancient and modern. When we view the design from a distance we imagine we see a blooming flower garden. The design would suit being used as a wall decoration using small tiles. The photo on the left shows the pattern laid out in floor tiles.
Repeating unit: 16 x 16.

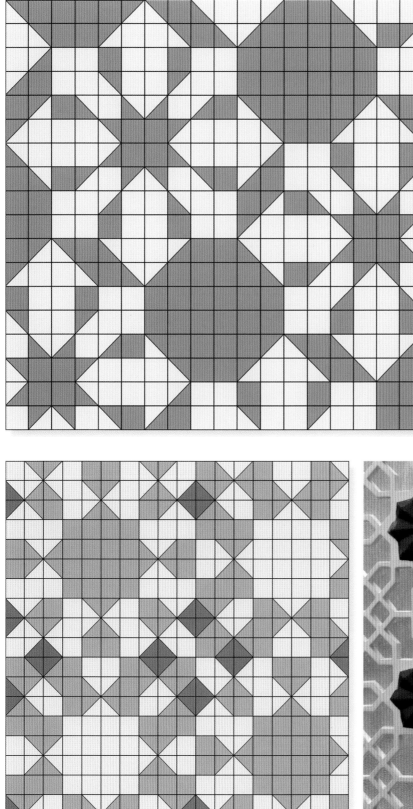

6.13 Arrowhead Star Formation

Another design suitable for use with small tiles on a feature wall, this drawing simply repeats the classic arrowhead star until we are fooled into thinking we can see circles on the square grid. If used as a floor pattern, it would be fun to follow the contradicting arrows. (See drawing 7.39 for the motif of the arrowhead star.)

6.14 Octagon Star Mass

Another classic Middle Eastern design, this drawing features a "rotated square" star surrounded by an elaborate octagon. It is repeated many times, creating an interesting interplay of positive and negative colors. As a modern application the design is found on the metal and glass gate (from Satwa, Dubai, U.A.E.) pictured above.
(See drawing 7.30 for the single motif that makes up the pattern.)
Repeating unit: 10 x 10.

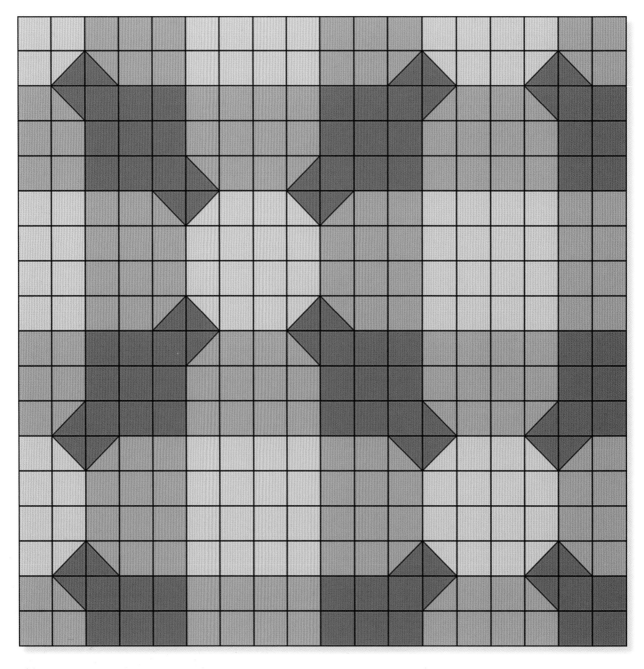

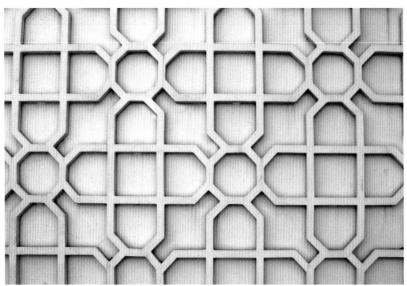

6.15 Jumeira Geometric

This very open geometric design is found on the solid iron gate (from Jumeira, Dubai, U.A.E.) shown in the photo on the left.
Repeating unit: 14 x 14.

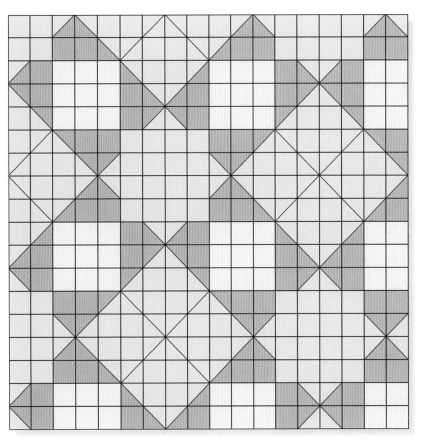

6.16 Ibn Battuta Windows

Inspired by a patterned skylight in a modern Middle Eastern shopping complex (Ibn Battuta Mall, Dubai, U.A.E.), shown in the photo above, this design is based on large stars placed on a square grid. The result looks like another play on a checkerboard pattern.

Repeating unit: 14 x 14.

6.17 Oud Metha Maze

This is a tile rendering of a design found on a modern mosque in Dubai, shown in the photo below right. The pattern is seen in plaster, wood and concrete, as it decorates walls, windows and doors.

Repeating unit: 14 x 14.

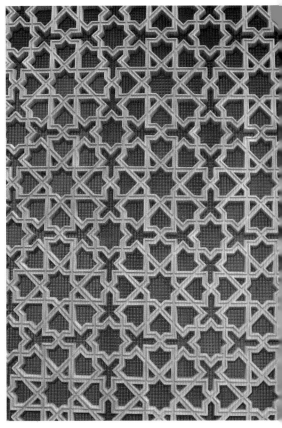

6.18 Classic Arabian Formation

This pattern is often seen in classic Islamic designs. They are usually so complex that it is hard to analyze them in detail. As with many of the drawings here, this is possibly the first time the design has been rendered into a square tile pattern. *Repeating unit: 14 x 14.*

6.19 Ibn Battuta Geometric

Inspired by a decorated ceiling in a modern Middle Eastern shopping mall (Ibn Battuta Mall, Dubai, U.A.E.), as shown in the photo above right, this design plays with intersecting lines that create diamonds and octagons. *Repeating unit: 12 x 12.*

6.20 Hexagon Weave

This apparently complex design was created by rotating long shapes around the edges of a hexagon. The resulting color scheme makes the whole design look like a weaving pattern.
Repeating unit: 6 x 12.

6.21 Brunei Geometric

This mass of hexagons and octagons around a "rotated square" star was inspired by a wooden door in the Jame Asr Hassanil Bolkiah Mosque in Brunei.
Repeating unit: 14 x 8.

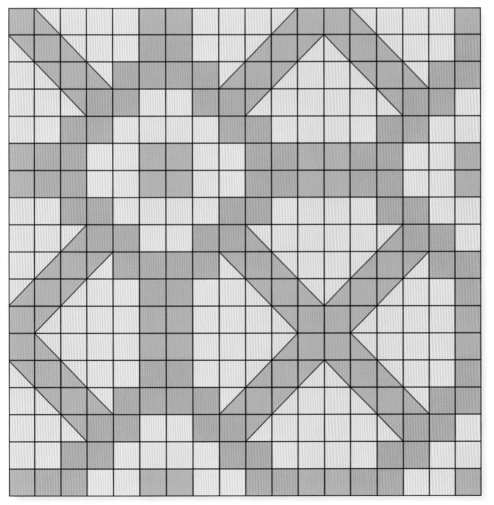

6.22 Dubai Deco

This design renders the wall design shown in the photo accompanying drawing 4.20 more accurately. Compare this with drawing 4.20.
Repeating unit: 12 x 12.

6.23 Complex Pinwheels

In addition to the complex tessellated designs we have seen in this chapter, you can move slightly away from the continuous checkerboard idea by inserting an odd, un-tessellated shape and then building around it. This drawing is an example. We can see here that a small star and octagon have been inserted into a central shape and the pinwheels then build around it. Again, the possibilities are endless for such designs.

Distorting a tessellation by inserting an odd shape leads us to the next chapter. The section focuses on building a pattern from a central focal point, producing what can be termed a "medallion" design. Such designs can be completely different from what we have seen so far, or, alternately, they can be incorporated into tessellation patterns, as in the example above.

Chapter 7

Medallion patterns

Moving completely away from the continuous checkerboard grid idea, we can examine patterns that have a basic "medallion" style. This means that the pattern has a central focus and builds outward from there. This type of design is suitable for features, such as the central part of a courtyard or large lounge, or a feature wall. Small medallion patterns or motifs are useful as space fillers. They can also be used as inserts to add interest to a plain tiled floor.

With the medallion-style pattern, we can often discern lines in the basic structure that radiate outward from the center. The pattern then begins from these lines.

The following pages show some medallion-style patterns.

7.1 Lightning Flash

7.2 Classic Eight-Pointed Star
This motif is the basis of many Middle Eastern geometric designs.

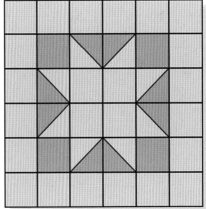

7.3 Dazzle Tunnel

This design is based on a concrete wall in Jumeira, Dubai, U.A.E., shown in the photo on the left.

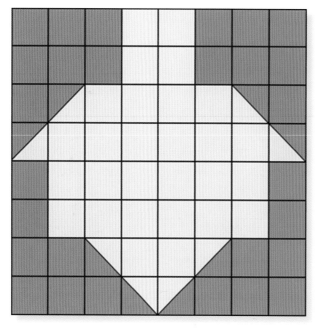

7.4 Leaf

See drawing 3.12 for this leaf motif en masse. The photo above shows the pattern laid out in tiles.

7.5 Spiral

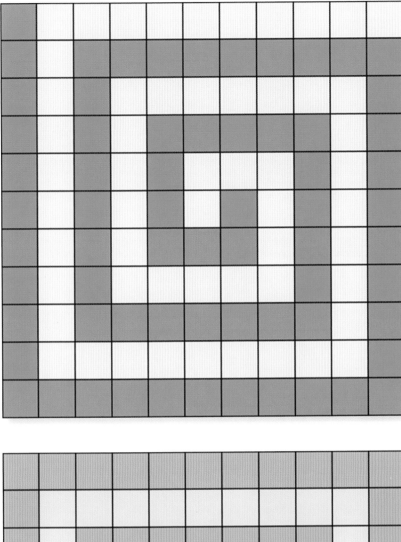

7.6 Diagonal Cross

This basic cross motif is found in many geometric patterns. See drawing 4.1 for an example.

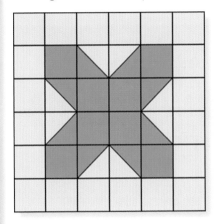

7.7 Nested Squares

7.8 Vertical Cross

This cross motif is found in many geometric designs. See drawing 4.2 for an example.

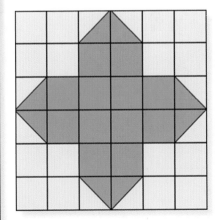

7.9 Warped Checkerboard

A design like this can create an interesting surprise element inserted into a normal checkerboard grid.

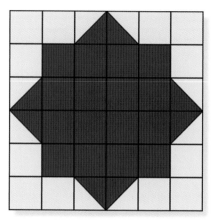

7.10 Rotated-Square Star

This motif is the basis of many Middle Eastern geometric designs. See drawing 4.1 for an example.

7.11 Triangle Checkerboard

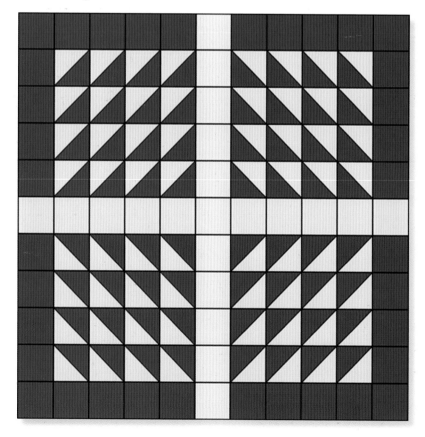

7.12 Six-Pointed Star Flower

See drawing 4.11 for this flower motif en masse. It is the only way to make a six-pointed star with square tiles.

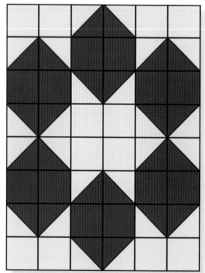

7.13 Triangle Tunnel

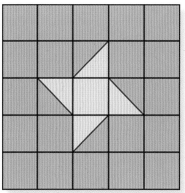

7.14 Four-Pointed Star

This little star motif is found in many geometric designs. See drawing 4.3 for an example.

7.15 Eight-Point Star with Nested Squares

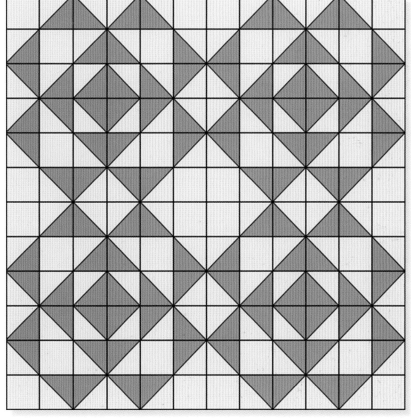

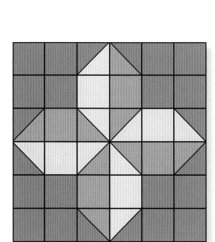

7.16 Straight Cross

This motif is part of several classic designs. See drawing 4.7 for an example.

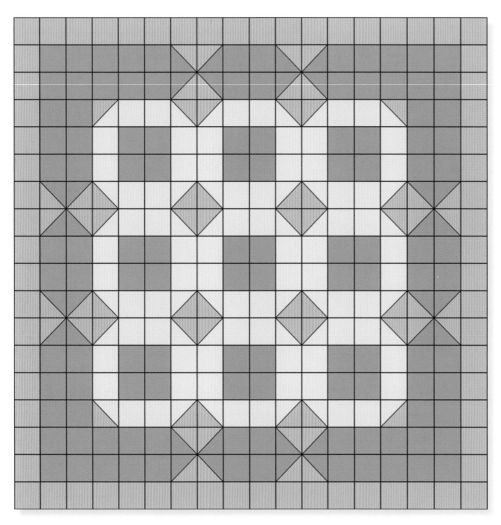

7.17 Fatima Square

The motif on the left was inspired by a design in brass with painted Arabesque detail inside the shapes. It is found on the wall of the Haja Fatima Mosque in Kuwait.

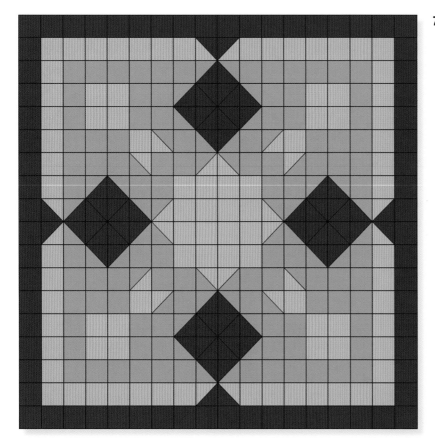

7.18 Arrow Formation

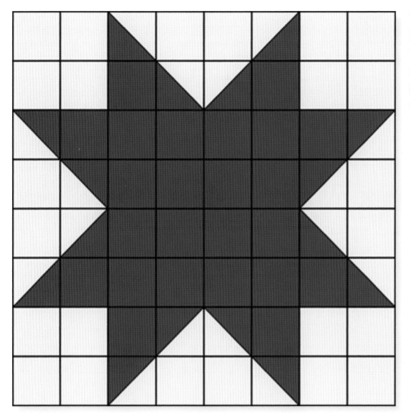

7.19 Large Classic Eight-Pointed Star

This motif forms the central focus of many geometric designs. See drawing 5.19 for an example. It is the larger version of drawing 7.2.

7.20 Two-Toned Large Classic Star

This is the same star as in drawing 7.19, but with dividing lines that make eight distinct segments. It is perhaps the most commonly seen star design in tile patterns worldwide.

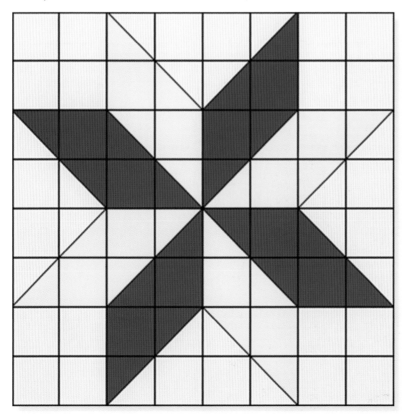

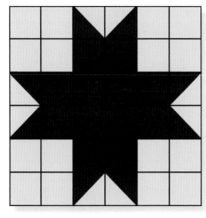

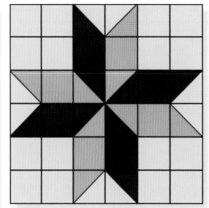

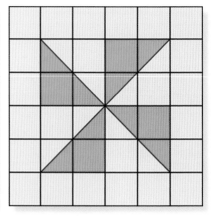

7.21 Straight Star
See drawings 5.23 and 5.24 for this motif en masse.

7.22 Segmented Straight Star
This is the same as drawing 7.21, but with lines separating the star into eight segments.

7.23 Pinwheel
This shows a pinwheel shape. If a smaller version is required, just the four central squares can be used.

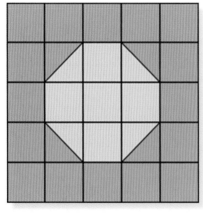

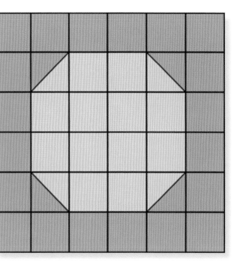

7.25 Medium Octagon

7.24 Smallest Octagon

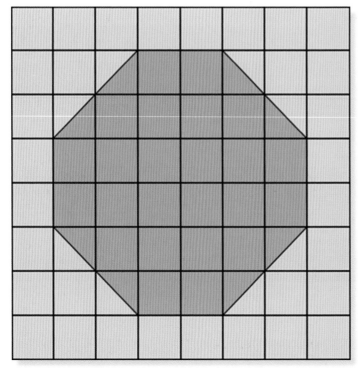

7.26 Large Octagon
Drawings 7.24, 7.25 and 7.26 demonstrate the basic octagon motifs that can be achieved with square tiles. Of course, we can make bigger octagons by continuing in the same fashion.

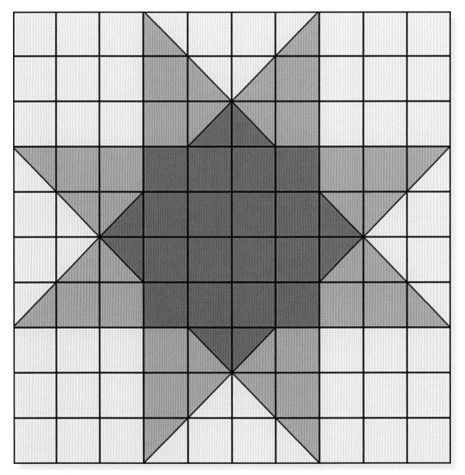

7.27 Large Complex Eight-Pointed Star

This is a commonly used complex star motif. It is a star built around another star. See drawing 6.6 for an example.

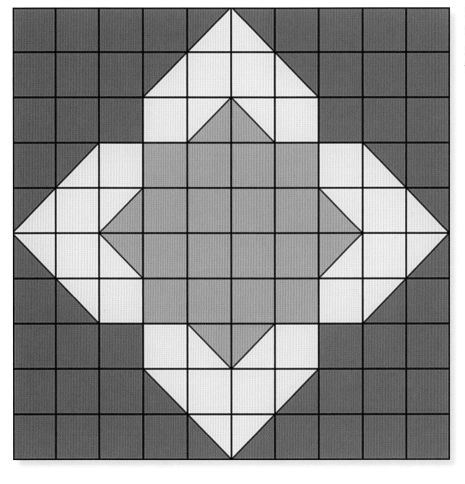

7.28 Framed Rotated Square Star

See drawings 5.3 and 5.16 for this motif en masse.

7.29 Diamond Medallion

This motif was inspired by an old metal door in a Middle Eastern wall, as seen in the photo below, left.

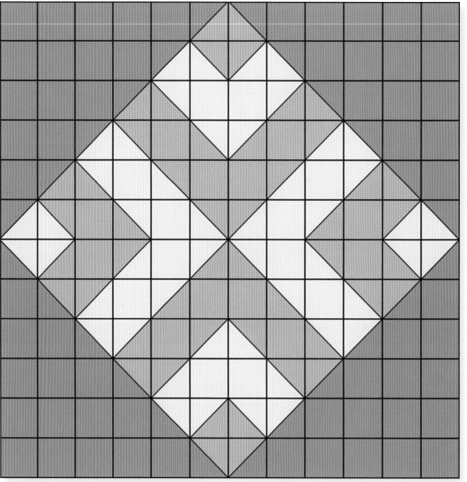

7.30 Octagon Star

This very balanced design with its tessellation-style pattern can be reproduced in tiles, as shown in the photo below left. Almost any tessellated design can provide various motifs to isolate and use on their own. This octagon star is another classic and would look great as a central feature in a tiled room or patio.

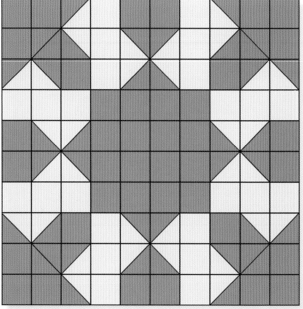

7.32 Middle East Motif

This pattern was lifted from a colorful Middle Eastern table runner, shown in the photo above right. What was a small design on fabric becomes quite a large design in tiles.

7.33 Cotton Spools Motif

This design uses the shapes in drawing 5.9 but arranges them into a single motif. See also drawing 10.43 for the same shapes used as a border. One could, for example, place the above design in the center of a floor and surround it by a similarly styled border.

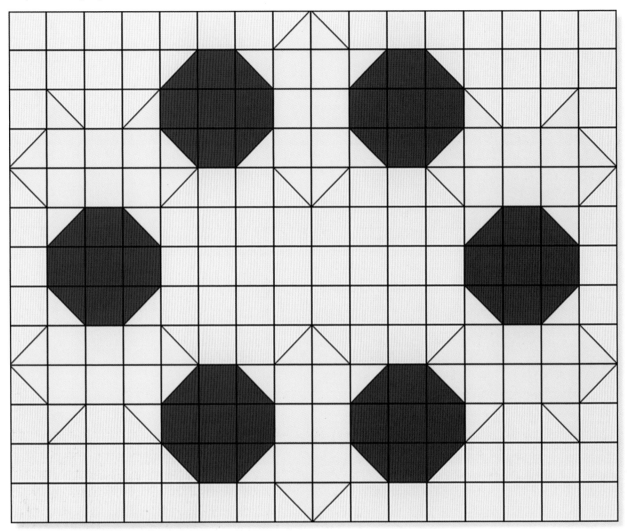

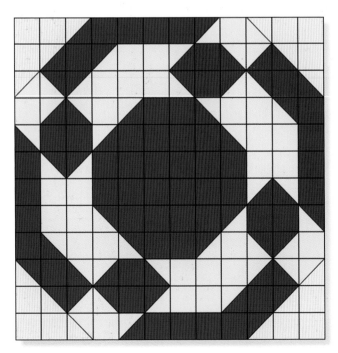

7.34 Octagon Medallion

This pleasant motif built up of nested octagons appears to be rotating because of the angled lines coming off the small hexagons.

7.35 Nested Squares with Octagon

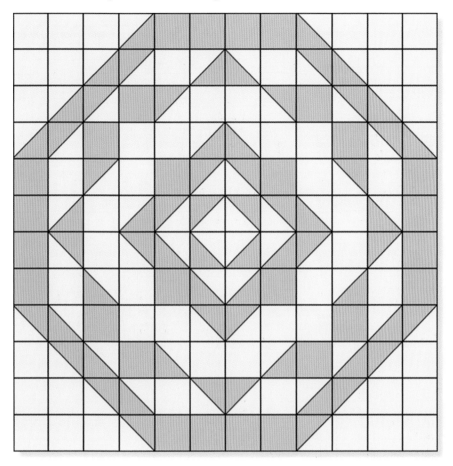

7.36 Gridlocked Octagons
This design was lifted from the tessellated pattern shown in drawing 6.3. The play of positive and negative colors here is pleasing to observe.

7.37 Twisted Square

A fun play with squares, rectangles and diamonds, this motif would sit well in an exterior courtyard.

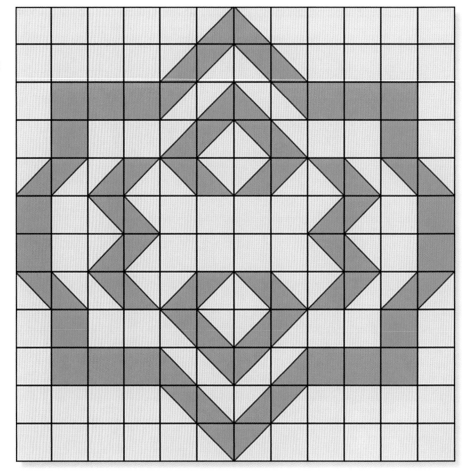

7.38 Scary Star

Another fun pattern for a central piece, this sharp design is best suited to a flooring situation.

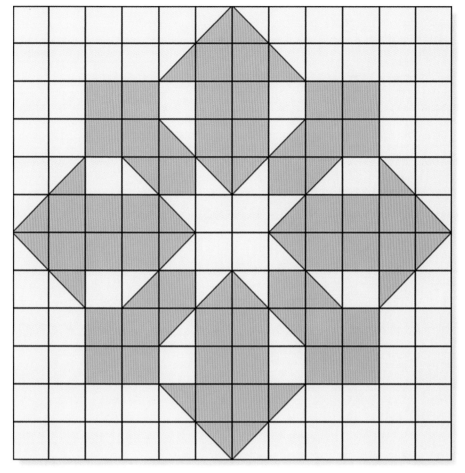

7.39 Arrowhead Star

This motif forms part of many classic Middle Eastern designs. See, for example, drawings 6.12 and 6.13.

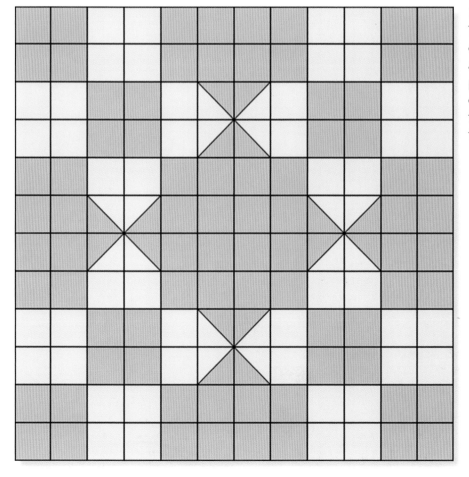

7.40 Checkerboard Star

This design distorts a checkerboard pattern to add an interesting focal point. Compare this with drawing 5.4, which shows the effect of having the stars throughout the design.

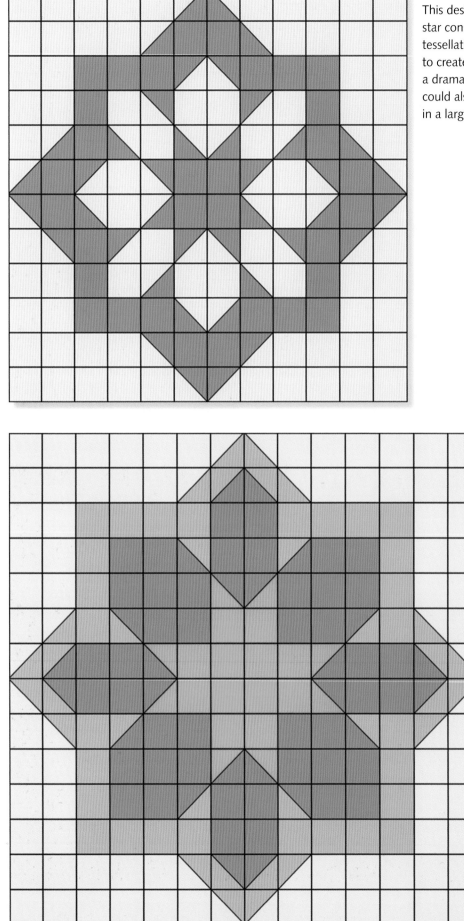

7.41 Framed Hexagon Star
This design takes the hexagonal star constantly found in Islamic tessellation patterns and frames it to create a pleasing motif. It makes a dramatic stand-alone pattern and could also be repeated periodically in a large tiled area.

7.42 Large Hexagonal Star
This is a larger version of drawing 7.41. The larger star at the center expands the whole design.

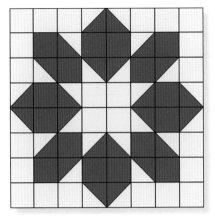

7.43 Simple Hexagonal Star

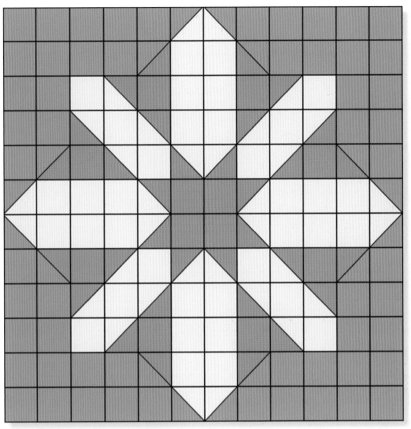

7.44 Long Hexagonal Star
This shows another variation on the hexagonal star theme.

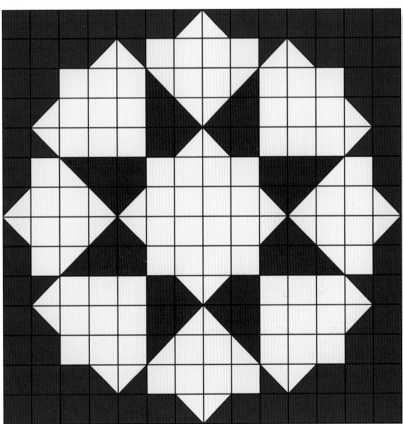

7.45 Pointed Pentagon Star
This wonderful star motif is also central to many Islamic geometric designs, such as on this metal coffee pot.

7.46 Layered Star

7.47 Nested Squares Star

Drawings 7.46 and 7.47 show more variations on star motifs. Both work on apparent layers of stars and squares.

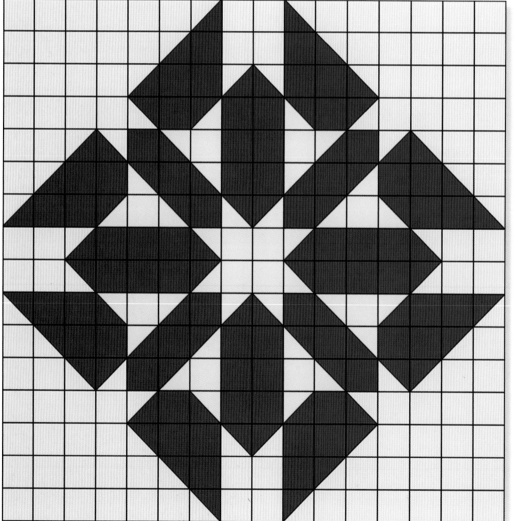

7.48 Winged Star

This large star motif leads us onto the next chapter, which is devoted entirely to larger star patterns.

Chapter 8

Star designs

The medallion-style pattern lends itself well to the building of various star-shaped designs. Traditionally, Islamic or Middle Eastern geometry abounds with star patterns, from four-pointed stars right up to 12-pointed stars and more. The square grid layout of tiles really only allows the creation of four- and eight-pointed star patterns. However, there are many variations of these. The following pages show a number of patterns based on stars. Many of these are classics designs and can be found on walls, windows, doors and floors throughout the Middle East.

8.1 Arrowhead Star

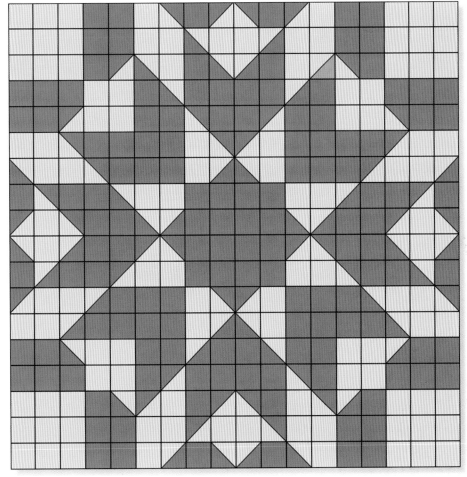

8.2 Pointed Pentagon Star

This is a pleasingly balanced design that is found both in complex Middle Eastern tessellation-style patterns as well as in simple motifs. Note the corners of the drawing, which show how the pattern can be repeated in diagonal directions. The beauty of being able to have this classic design grace any tiled space, without the use of specialized mosaic techniques, perfectly illustrates what this book is all about. (The photo shows a tiled courtyard at the Prophet's Mosque, Medina, Saudi Arabia.)

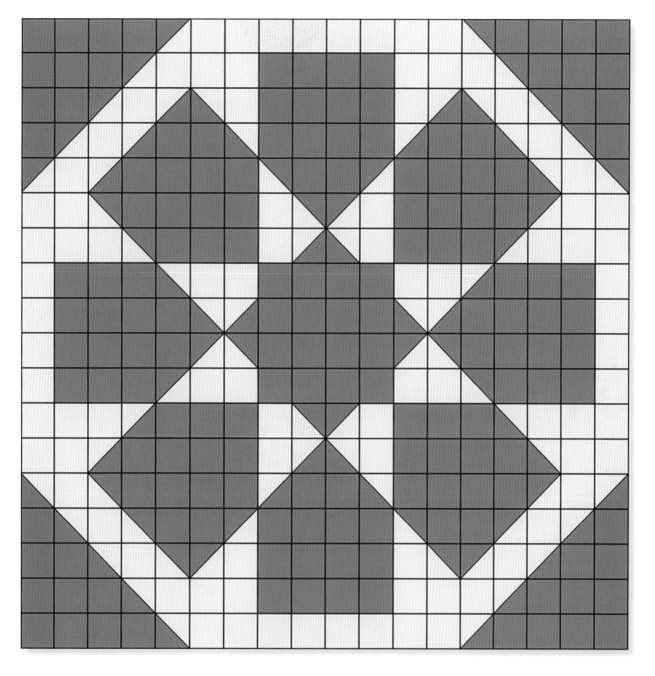

8.3 Pentagon Star

Once again, pentagons surrounding a complex star, as featured in many geometric designs. The lattice shown in the photo on the right (from Ibn Battuta Mall, Dubai, U.A.E.) has distorted pentagons that incorporate small stars into the pattern.

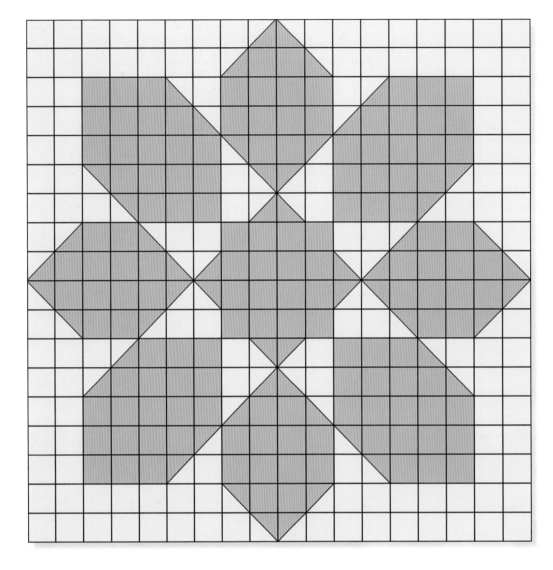

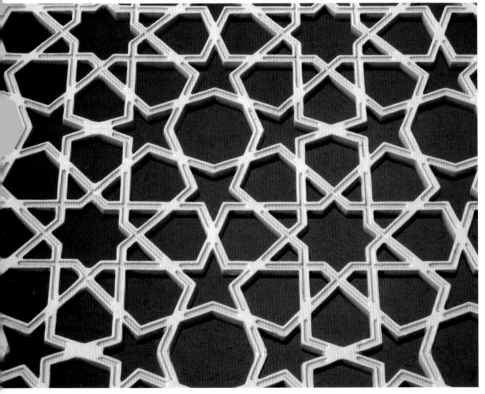

8.4 Classic Hexagon Star

This star is another classic, found in dozens of Middle Eastern decorations. Note the difference between this design and drawings 7.42, 7.43 and 7.44, in which the internal stars are smaller and simpler. The photo on the left shows this star embedded in a complex metal grille design (from Satwa, Dubai, U.A.E.). It would look spectacular to use such a grille on a fence with the star design on a tiled patio nearby.

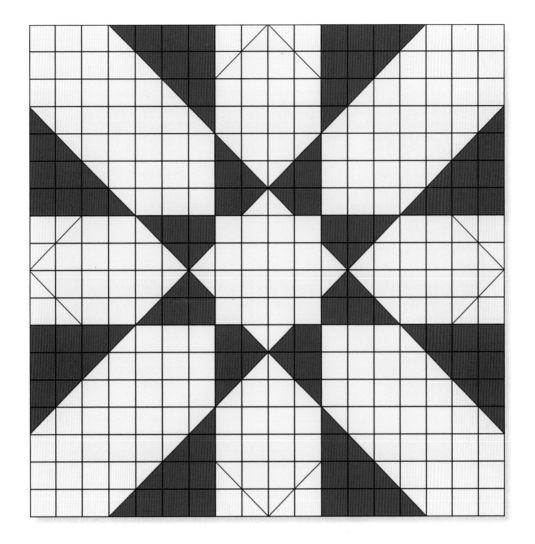

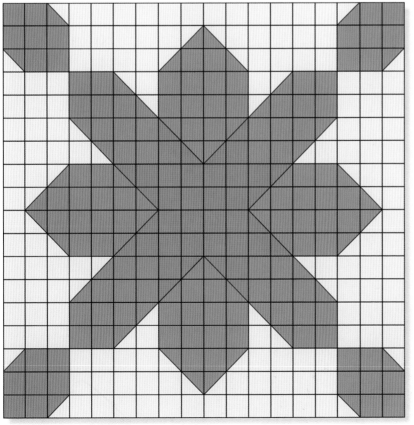

8.5 Satwa Hexagon Star

This drawing follows the complex pattern shown in the grille in the photo opposite. If it is repeated horizontally and vertically, large triangles and more stars will form in the connecting spaces.

8.6 Simple Hexagon Star

A larger version of drawing 7.43, this design shows how the hexagon star can be repeated from each diagonal corner if desired.

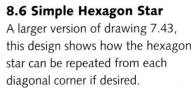

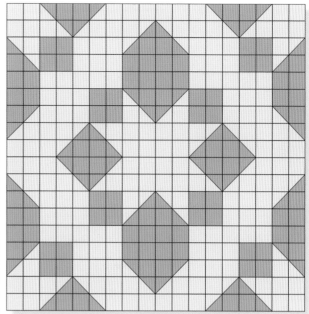

8.8 Polygon Star

A simpler star surrounded by squares, diamonds and hexagons, this drawing also shows how the central design can be repeated in all directions if desired.

8.7 Square Star

This time the same classic star shape as in drawing 8.1 is surrounded by squares. The internal design can stand alone or be framed in an octagon, as shown here.

8.9 Diamond Star

A larger simple star is connected here to a grid of double diamonds.

8.10 Classic Medallion Star

This segmented star, framed in pentagons that give it a floral appearance, is a common tiling design worldwide.

8.11 Three-Dimensional Star

The shading in this star gives the illusion of a three-dimensional figure.

8.12 Triple Star

This design has three stars superimposed on each other. The central portion has an interesting three-dimensional effect.

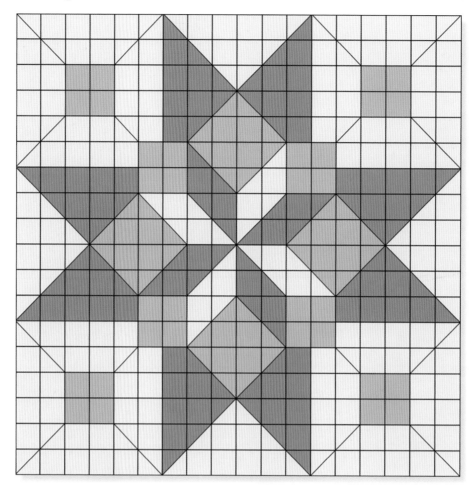

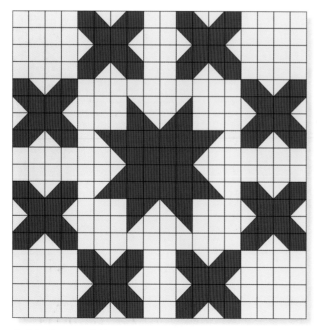

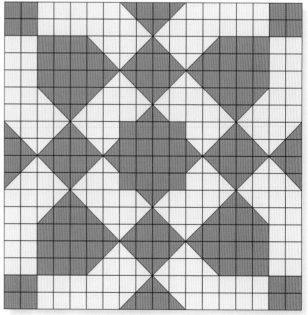

8.13 Crossed Star

This highly symmetrical star design is simple yet appealing. If it is repeated, the familiar "rotated square" star appears in the corners.

8.14 Marrakech Star

This design, with a small star inserted into a tilted checkerboard, is originally from Marrakech in Morocco.

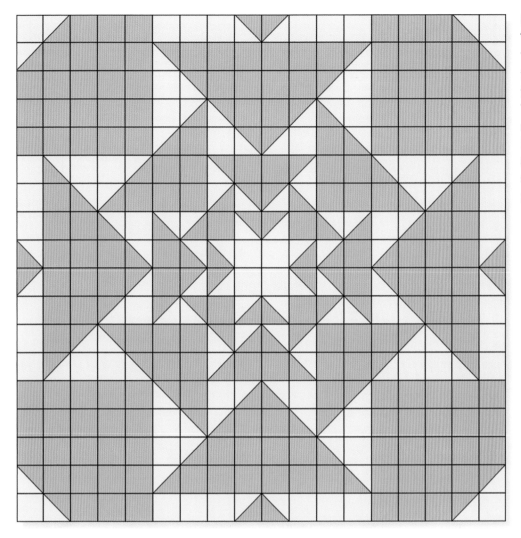

8.15 Expanding-Triangles Star

This design gives the impression of a triangle explosion. The small central star is surrounded by triangles that are doubling in size with each progressive layer.

8.16 Rotating-Triangles Star

In this design a small central "pinwheel" star begins the pattern. It is made from a square with triangles built onto it. Successive layers continue the rule and enlarge in size. The end result gives an impression of rotation, movement and growth.

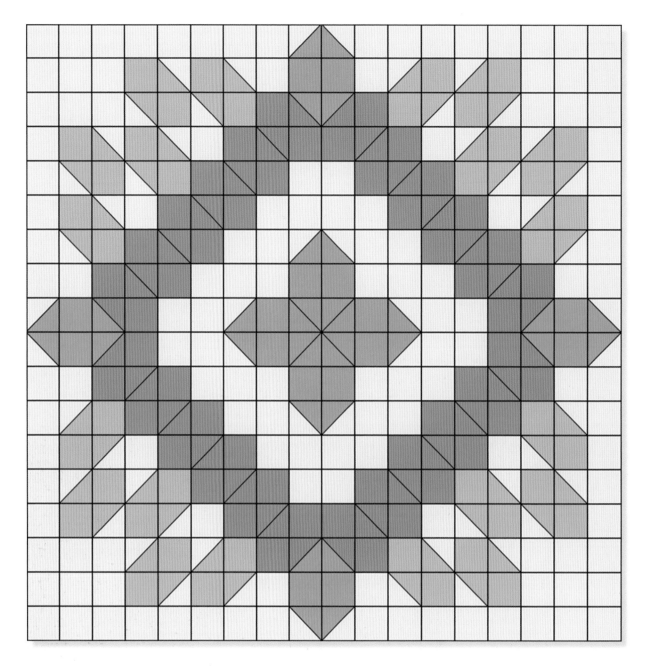

8.17 Hexagon Star Explosion
This fun design builds a starburst pattern using only hexagons.

8.18 Blazing Sun
Finally in this chapter we have a "real" star, the sun itself!

Chapter 9

Line designs

A completely different approach can be to use tiles to represent line patterns. These patterns often need at least three colors to show where one line laps over another or to distinguish one continuous line from another. If the tiles are laid on a floor, it can be fun to physically follow a trail while walking around the design. Again, many Middle Eastern designs can be adapted and used in this type of tile work.

The following pages show some examples of line designs, although many more could be invented.

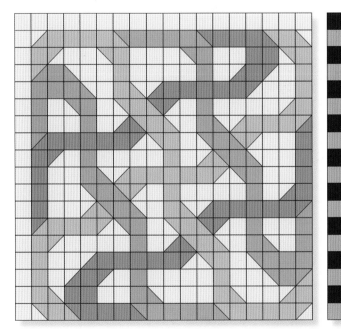

9.1 Crazy Roads

This drawing is a good example of a "woven" line design rendered in square tiles. Each line alternately overlaps and then goes behind other lines as they meet and cross.

9.2 Square Weave

Here a simple "woven" square makes a dramatic motif, highlighted by the extra framing around it.

Tiled roadway wall, Deira, Dubai, U.A.E.

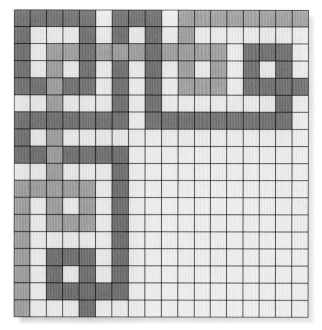

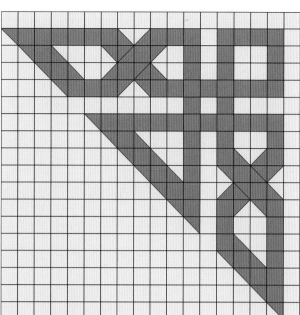

9.3 Loop the Loops

Loop designs like this one are useful in corners and as borders. There are many variations. See chapter 11 for more ideas.

9.4 Celtic Corner

This woven triangular design is useful for a corner feature. If we follow the line, we see that it is actually one piece that loops back onto itself. Children would enjoy following this type of pattern on a tiled floor.

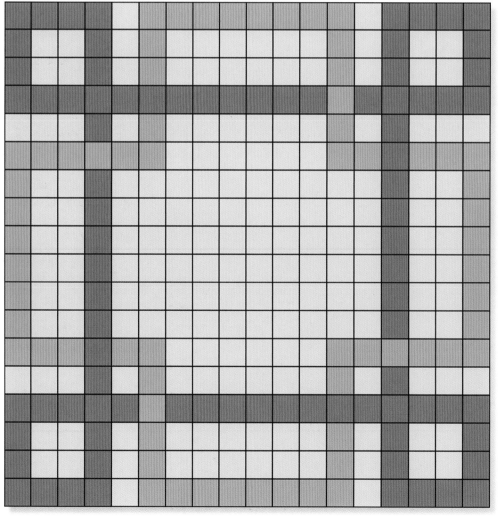

9.5 Egyptian Looped Border

This Egyptian design is an example of how to make a complete border using weaving and looping lines in the tiles. It is simple yet effective for framing a central area.

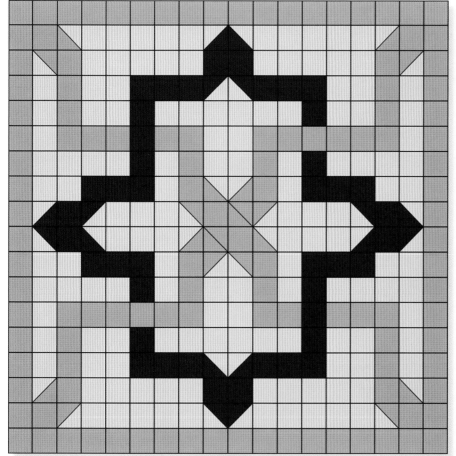

9.6 Damascus Diamond Weave

Here a central space is framed and filled with the woven line design. The design comes from Damascus in Syria.

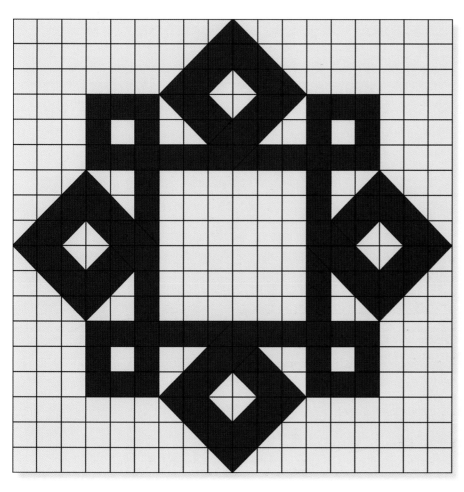

9.7 Tunisian Looped Square

This is a classic Islamic motif, originating in Tunisia and often found carved on walls, but it is not often seen in tiles! The size of some of the loops has had to be distorted in order to fit the square tile grid, but the beauty of the design remains.

9.8 Stairway to Heaven

This is a tile rendering of a classic Maori design seen on tukutuku (woven flax) panels in New Zealand.

9.9 Kuwaiti Curves

This pleasingly symmetrical woven-line design was inspired by carved wooden wall panels in the library of the Haja Fatima Mosque in Kuwait. We see that there are two woven strands in the pattern, and, if desired, we could use differently colored tiles to highlight this.

This is another line design suitable for framing the central area of a tiled courtyard or patio. We can imagine a fountain placed at the center or perhaps an outdoor dining table.

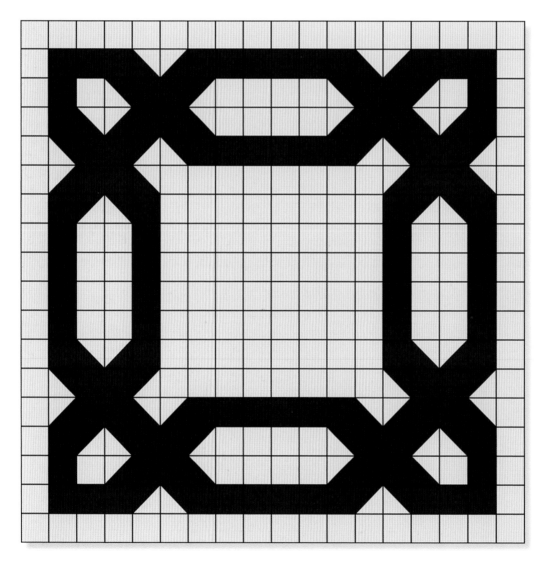

The following chapter elaborates on the idea of frames and borders, presenting many more possibilities for decorative edgings using tiles.

Chapter 10

Border designs

The use of tiled borders has endless possibilities. They can be very effective on the edges of courtyards or along garden walls. They can be installed in kitchens and bathrooms and along the tops of counters or skirting panels. They can surround a central rug on a lounge floor. An entrance or hallway could also be greatly enhanced by an eye-catching border.

As with the choice of any pattern, we need to consider the width of the border in the project, taking into consideration the size of the tiles we will use.

There are many classic border designs that we can render into tiled patterns, from the well-known Greek and Byzantine decorations, through the vast Islamic collection and on into the many patterns used by Pacific Islanders, Native Americans, Africans and others.

Many borders can be created by picking out a strip from a larger design, as described in chapter 2. This would be useful if we were to choose a main tiling design, say for the center of a courtyard, and then put a thin border around the edge to complement it.

Many of the designs we have already seen can be adapted into borders in this way. Some of the examples below have been created from "parent" patterns of earlier designs, and, in these cases, the relevant reference is given. Some of the examples below are based on line designs, similar to those in the previous chapter but more suited to borders.

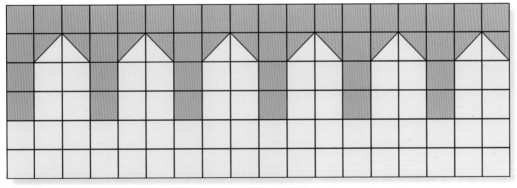

10.1 Pointed Arch

This design is, of course, inspired by what we see along the tops of medieval buildings, as well as many modern mosques.

10.2 Diamonds

This design is exemplified by the mosaic tiled wall pictured (from Dubai, U.A.E).

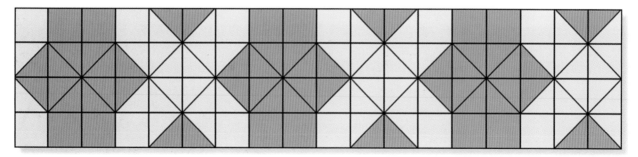

10.3 Triangles

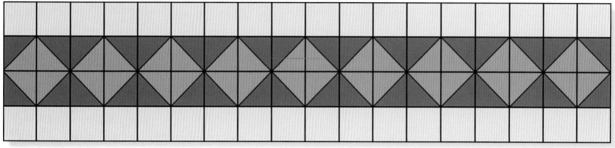

10.4 Diagonal Crosses

See drawing 4.18 for this design en masse.

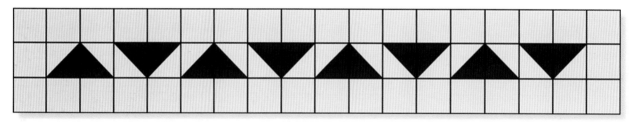

10.5 Diamond Flowers

See drawing 5.11 for this design en masse.

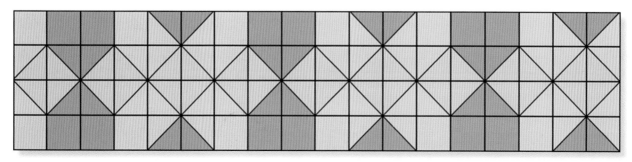

10.6 Framed Diamonds

See drawing 5.10 for this design en masse.

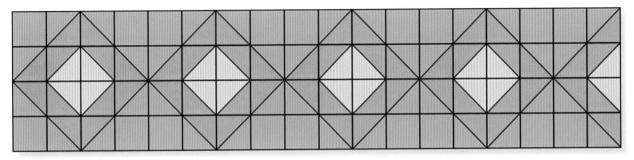

10.7 Large Triangles

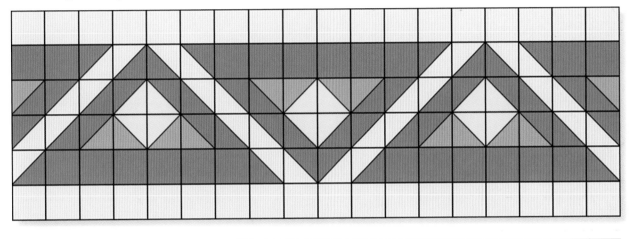

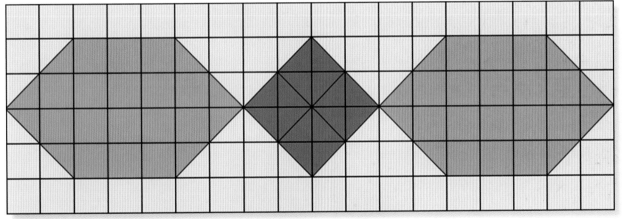

10.8 Diamond and Hexagon

This border is often used to decorate the outside of modern Middle Eastern buildings, such as the one pictured on the left (in Dubai, U.A.E.).

10.9 Two-Strand Weave

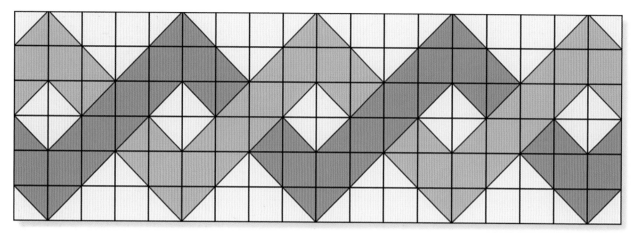

10.10 Three-Strand Weave

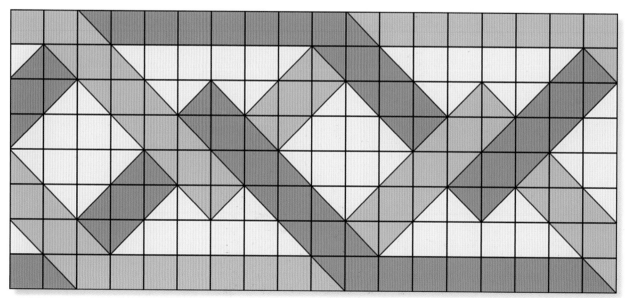

10.11 Four-Strand Weave

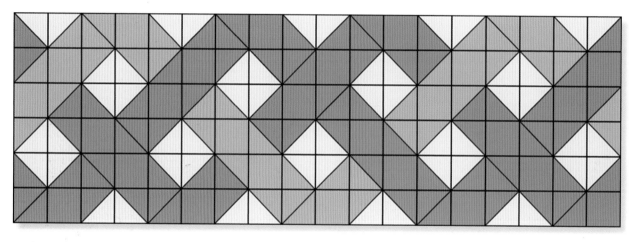

10.12 Star Weave

10.13 Square Arch

This design can be seen in the photo of a city building in Deira, Dubai, U.A.E., at bottom.

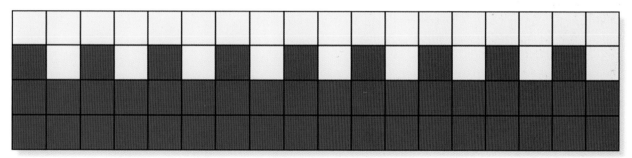

10.14 Hexagons

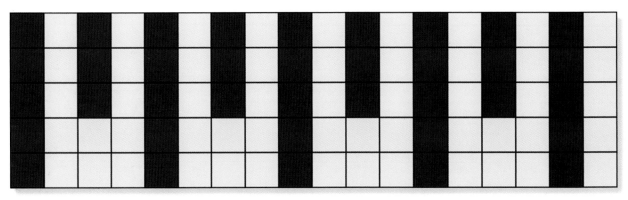

10.15 Qaboos Lines

This simple vertical line border decorates a stone arch in the Grand Mosque of Sultan Qaboos in Muscat, the Sultanate of Oman.

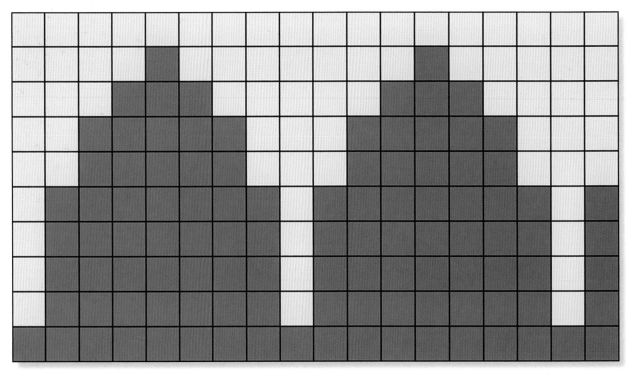

10.16 Fortification Arch

10.17 Bars Border

See drawing 5.15 for this border design en masse.

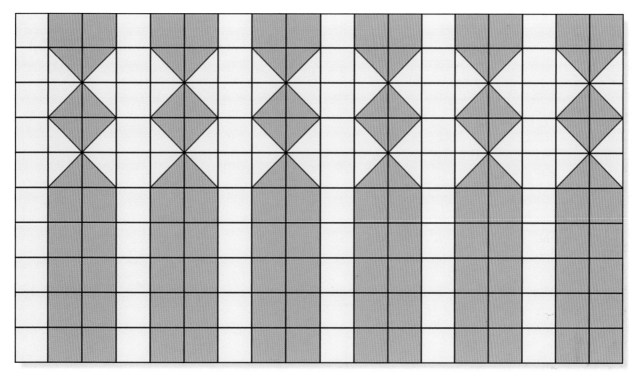

10.18 Grille Border

See drawing 5.14 for this border design en masse.

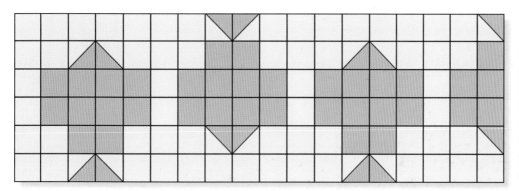

10.19 Lamps

This lamps border appears in an arch frieze in the Grand Mosque of Sultan Saeed bin Taimour in Oman. See drawing 5.30 for the design en masse.

10.20 Classic Rotated-Squares Border

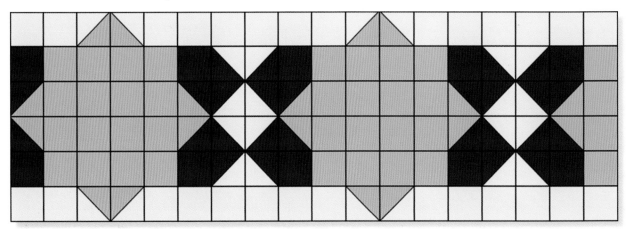

10.21 Sadeq Border

This border can be seen as a wall tile frieze in the Imam Sadeq Mosque in Bahrain. It only differs from drawing 10.4 in color scheme.

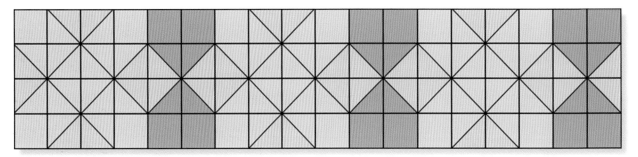

10.22 Qaboos Triangles

This design was inspired by a marble arched window frame in the Sultan Qaboos Mosque in Muscat, the Sultanate of Oman.

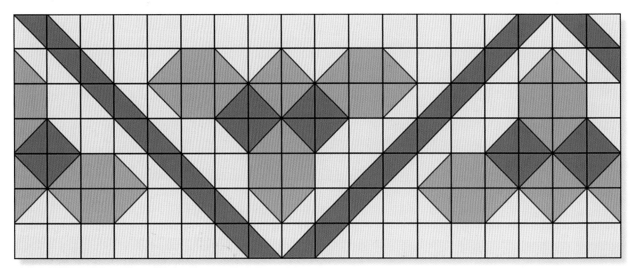

10.23 Qatari Classic

This border design came from a dome frieze in colored plaster work in the Mosque of Hamad bin Khalid bin Hamad al Thani in the State of Qatar. In the mosque, the rotated squares are filled with Arabic calligraphy, and the hexagons are filled with painted arabesque designs.

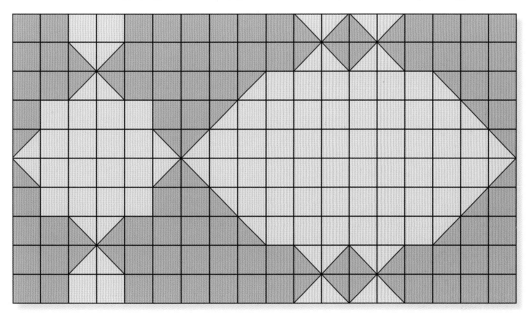

10.24 Moroccan Triangles

This simple but effective design was seen as a Moroccan gypsum frieze on the inside walls of the Grand Mosque in Kuwait.

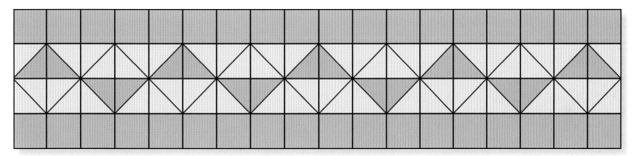

10.25 Kuwaiti Classic

This design is also taken from part of the Moroccan gypsum wall border in the Grand Mosque, Kuwait.

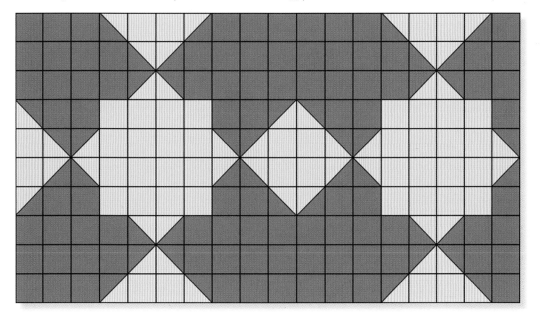

10.26 Woven Hexagons

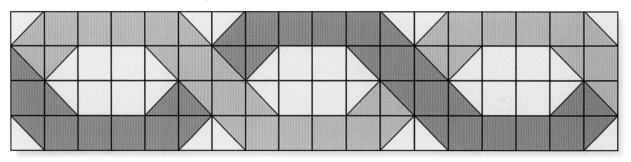

10.27 Fatima Frieze

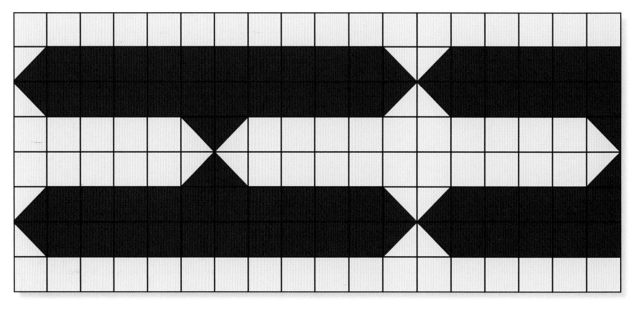

10.28 Woven Fatima Frieze

This border is seen as a wooden wall decoration in the Haja Fatima Mosque in Kuwait.
Drawing 10.27 is a simplified version of it.

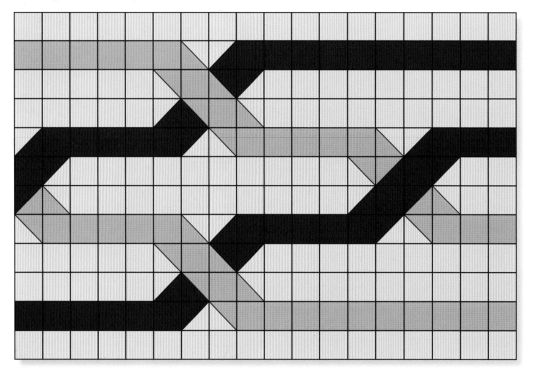

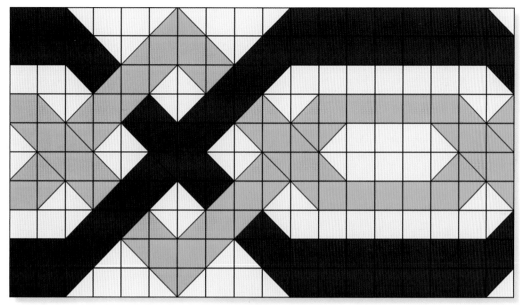

10.29 Classic Carpet Border

This four-strand woven pattern was inspired by a classic Middle Eastern carpet border, as seen in the photo on the right.

10.30 Celtic Curves

This ancient design crosses several cultures. An attractive version of it can be seen on the photo of an Arabian coffee pot accompanying drawing 7.45.

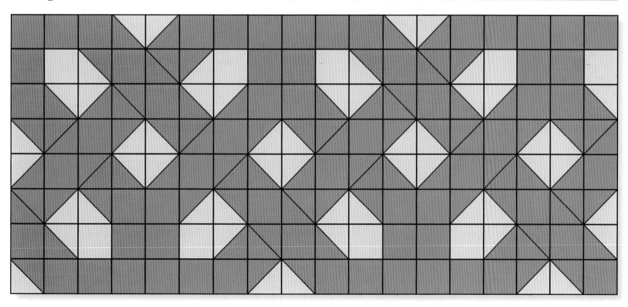

10.31 Classic Greek

10.32 Square Wave

10.33 Small Square Spiral
This design can be seen in the photo on the right of a school building in Dubai, U.A.E. See drawing 11.7 for this design en masse.

10.34 Large Square Spiral

Drawings 10.33 and 10.34 were inspired by concrete block friezes that are commonly seen on the tops of walls. The first border mimics the blocks closely, while in the second the scale is increased and the edges of the "blocks" are merged.

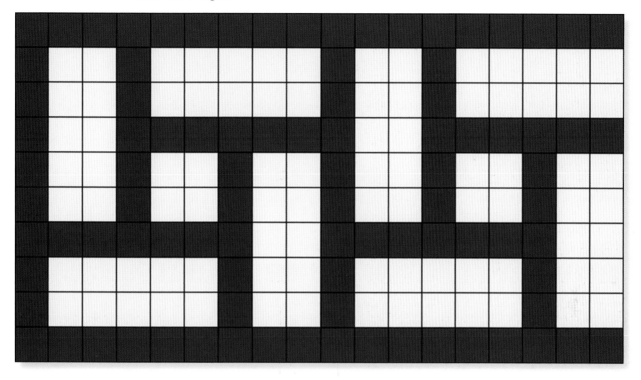

10.35 Interwoven Diamond

This woven diamond design was inspired by a simple plaster border on an apartment building. When we compare the drawing to the photo, we see how a woven pattern can add interest to an ordinary design.

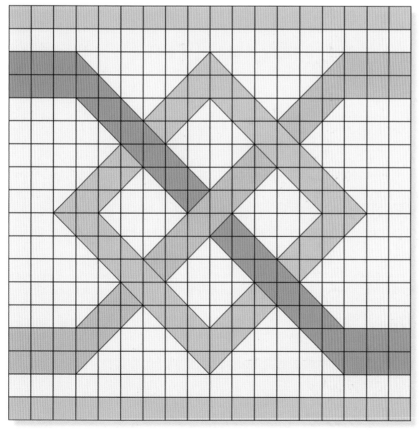

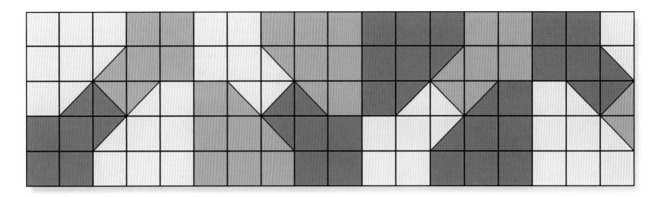

10.36 Crazy Arrows

See drawing 4.17 for this drawing en masse. The photo on the left shows the concrete wall frieze that inspired the design.

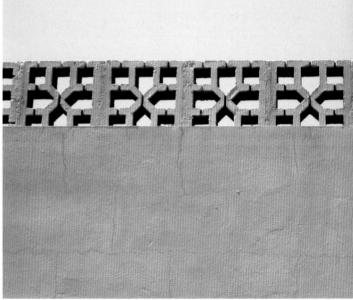

10.37 Blocked Pentagon Border

See drawing 5.12 for a version of this pattern en masse. The design was once again inspired by a concrete block wall frieze, shown in the photo on the right.

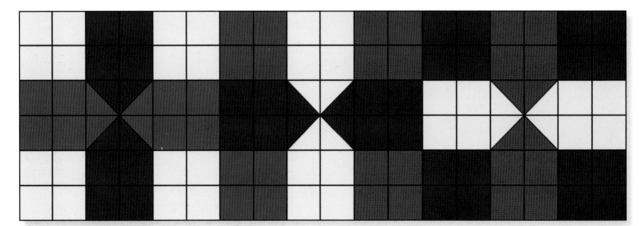

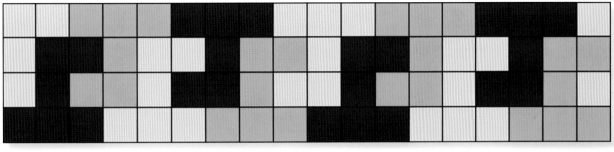

10.38 Jumeira Jays

This fun border came from an iron gate edging in Jumeira, Dubai, U.A.E.

10.39 Scarab Border

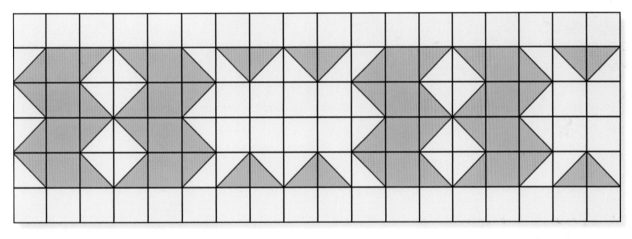

10.40 Rotated-Square Border

For an en masse version of this design see drawing 5.1.

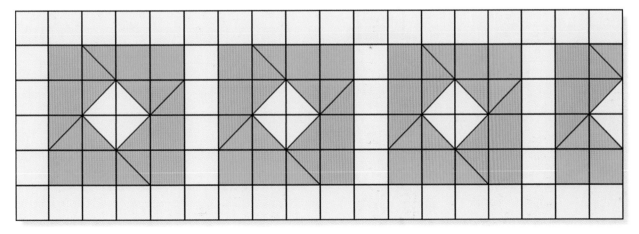

10.41 Star Brigade

For this star border en masse see drawing 5.2.

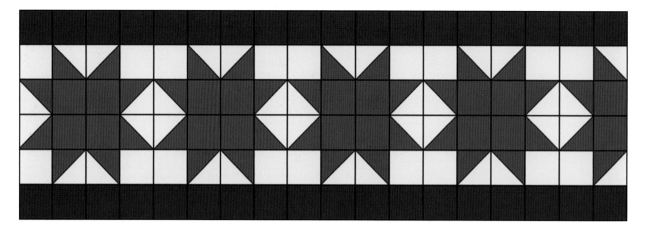

10.42 Trees Border

See drawing 4.12 for this design en masse.

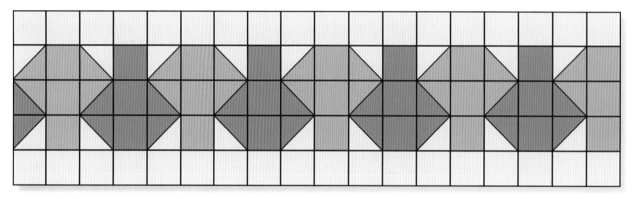

10.43 Cotton Spools Border

See drawing 5.9 for this border design en masse.

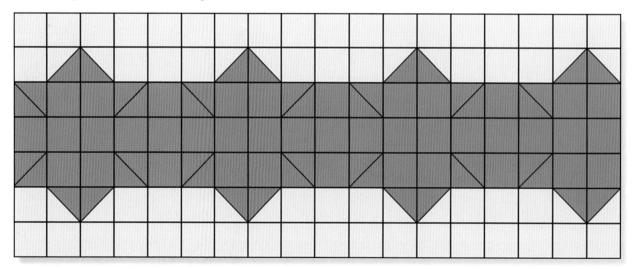

10.44 Hexagon Parade

See drawing 4.4 for this design en masse.

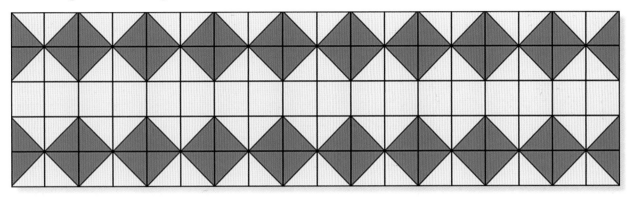

10.45 Pinwheel Border

See drawing 4.16 for this design en masse.

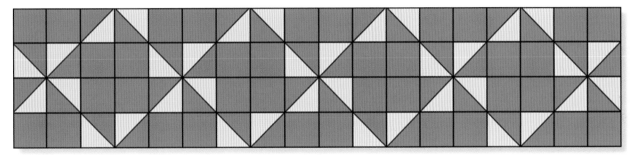

10.46 Balqiah Border

See drawing 5.17 for this design en masse.

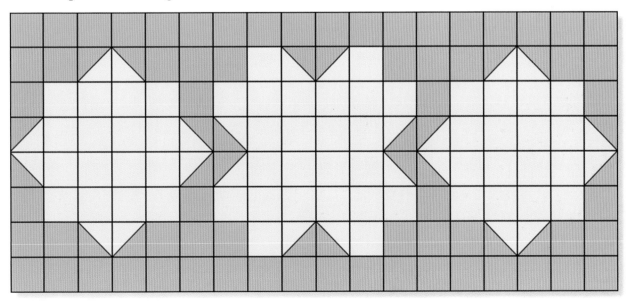

10.47 Hammerhead Border

See drawing 4.27 for this design en masse.

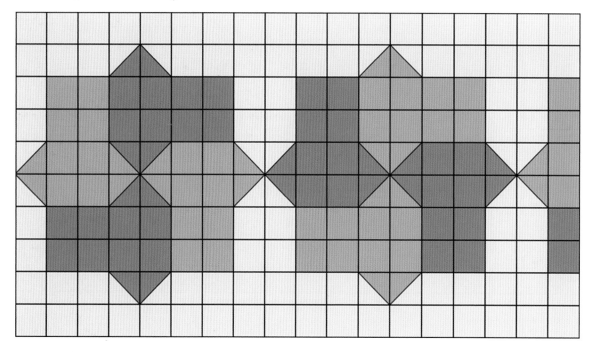

10.48 Dubai Diamonds

See drawing 4.20 for this design en masse.

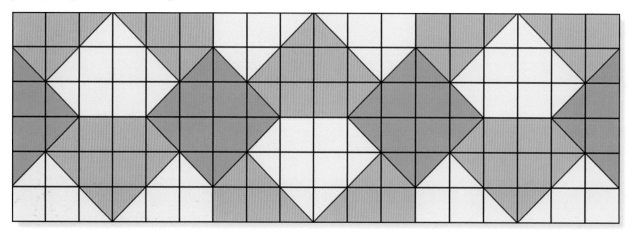

10.49 Bars Border

See drawing 4.21 for this design en masse.

10.50 Hexagon Weave Border

See drawing 4.25 for this design en masse.

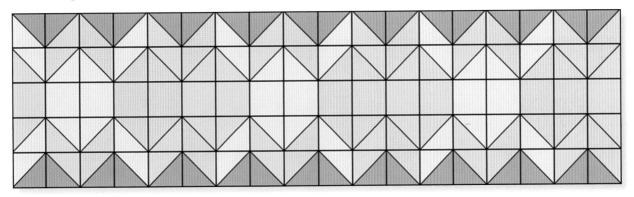

10.51 Triangle Strip

See drawing 3.8 for this design en masse.

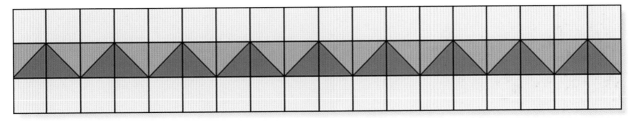

10.52 Big Triangle Strip

See drawing 3.8 for this design en masse.

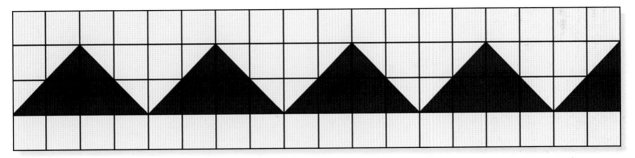

10.53 Zigzag

See drawing 3.9 for this design en masse.

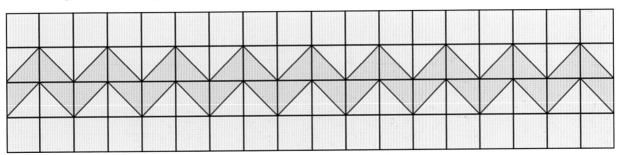

10.54 Big Zigzag

See drawing 3.9 for this design en masse.

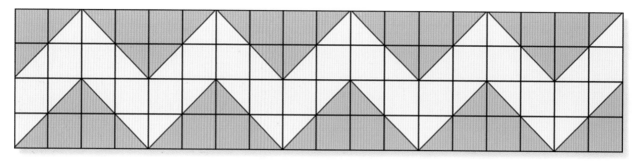

10.55 Hexagon Flower Border

See drawing 3.10 for this design en masse.

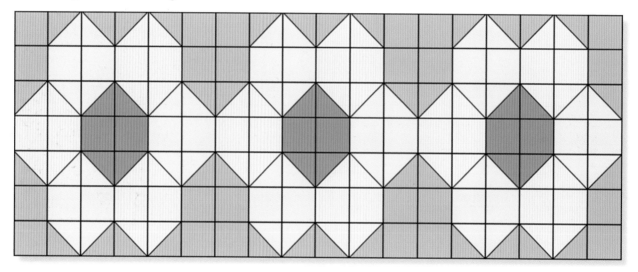

10.56 Medina Border

See drawing 3.13 for this design en masse.

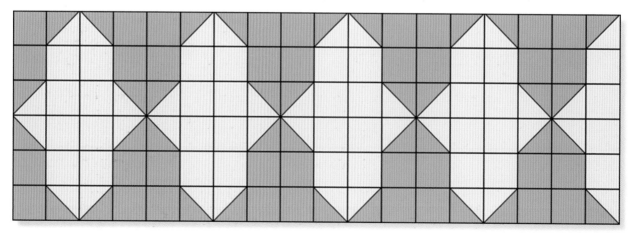

10.57 Horsemen Row

See drawing 3.19 for this design en masse.

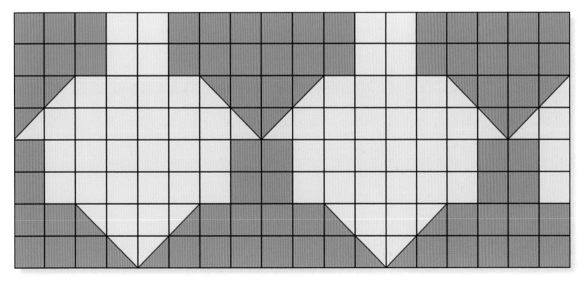

10.58 Insect Row

See drawing 3.17 for this design en masse.

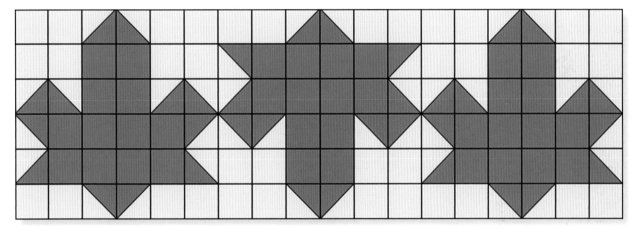

10.59 Leaf Row

See drawing 3.12 for this design en masse.

10.60 Arrowhead Border

See drawing 3.3 for this design en masse.

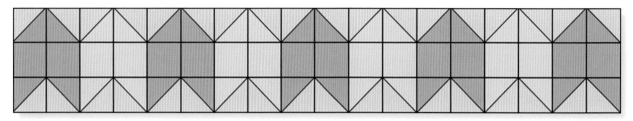

10.61 Azhar Stars

This design was inspired by concrete wall edging at the Al Azhar Mosque in Cairo, Egypt.

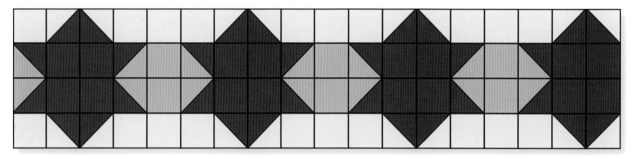

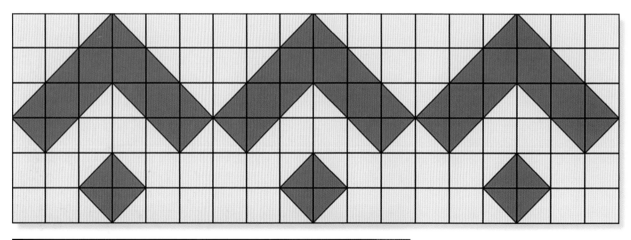

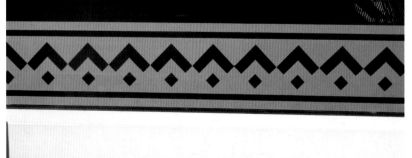

10.62 Wellington Hills

This is a tile rendering of a hills motif, shown in the photo on the left, by the designer of the entranceway to Wellington Mosque, New Zealand.

10.63 Diamond Grille Border

This design is reflected in the metal grille fence
pictured at bottom, from Satwa, Dubai, U.A.E.

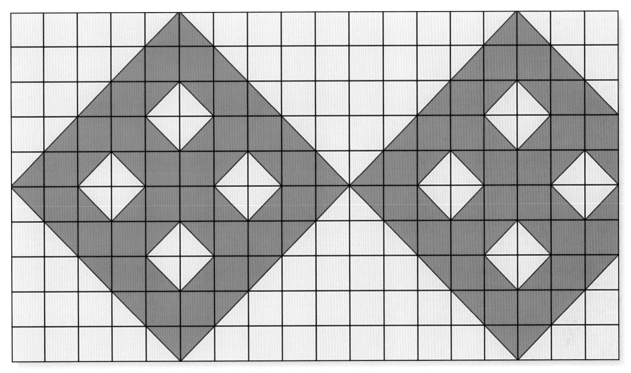

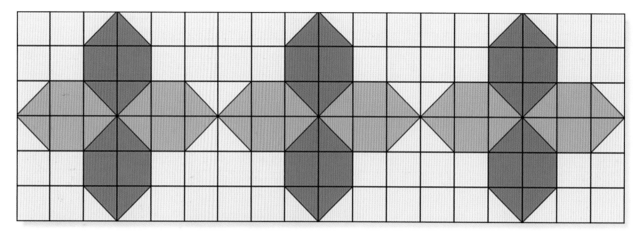

10.64 Straight Crosses

See drawing 4.7 for this design en masse. The frieze is seen in the pattern edging an iron gate (photo on the left).

10.65 Baqi Border

See drawing 4.2 for this design en masse. It is in fact very similar to the border shown in drawing 10.64 above, except that a different part of the pattern has been highlighted. The design was found on the mosaic tiled wall of Jannatul Baqi in Medina, Saudi Arabia, pictured on the right.

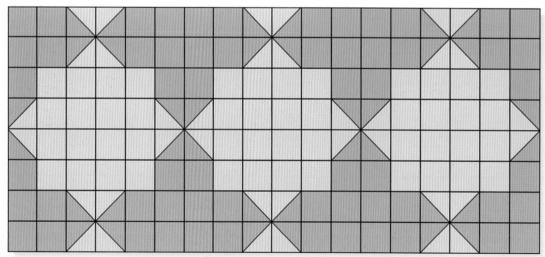

10.66 Brunei Border

This pleasing border is found on tiled walls of the Jame Asr Hassanil Bolkiah Mosque in Brunei.

10.67 Dancing Stars

See drawing 4.3 for this fun star design en masse.

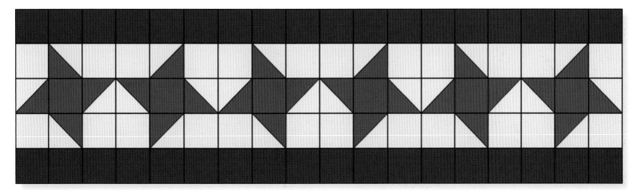

10.68 Whole-Square Dancing Stars

This design is found as the tiled frieze on a wall shown in the photo below. Viewing drawings 10.67 and 10.68 together illustrates the difference between the sharper image produced by diagonally cut tiles and the more blurry image produced by whole-square tile patterns. Both have their charms. Sometimes it is necessary to use whole square tiles because of tile size. It is difficult to cut very small tiles. If a border uses very small tiles then we see the pattern as if we are viewing it from a distance, and the blurring factor often beautifies it.

More whole-tile border patterns follow.

10.69 Whole-Square Diamond Border

10.70 Blurry Wave

10.71 Crescent Moons

Chapter 11 is devoted entirely to whole-square designs.

Chapter 11

Whole-square designs

Most of the previous designs have relied on cutting some tiles diagonally in order to complete the pattern. The drawings in this section are styled so that only whole squares are used. This produces a more blurred effect when viewing the pattern, which has a charm of its own.

Whole-square designs are particularly suited to small tiles, so that the pattern can be viewed more easily as a whole. Also, small tiles are difficult to cut, and thus we may be limited in terms of the choice of pattern. Nevertheless, many different designs can be dreamed up using whole squares. Chapter 10 has already introduced several whole-square tile border patterns. Chapter 9 has some whole-square line designs. Chapter 2 has a discussion of how any cross-stitch pattern can be rendered as a whole-square tile design.

The following pages show some more examples of whole-square designs.

11.1 Iranian Rotated Square

This is the whole-square version of the rotated-square star we have seen. It is highlighted by a frame in a similar style. Although we have stated that whole-square patterns are best suited to small tiles, in the photo the design is actually very large. It does, however, still rely on the viewer appreciating the pattern from a distance.

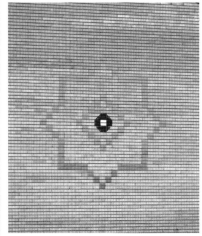

11.2 Star Windows 1

This design is found on a concrete grille in a modern mall, pictured below. The contrast between dark and light shapes is quite effective.

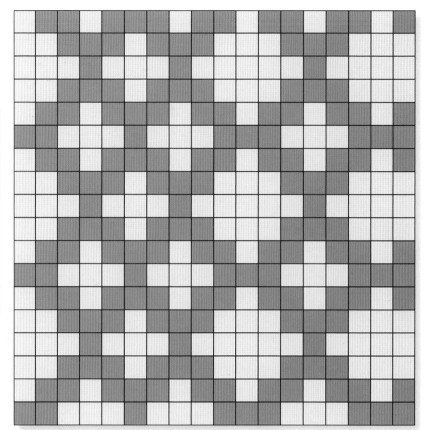

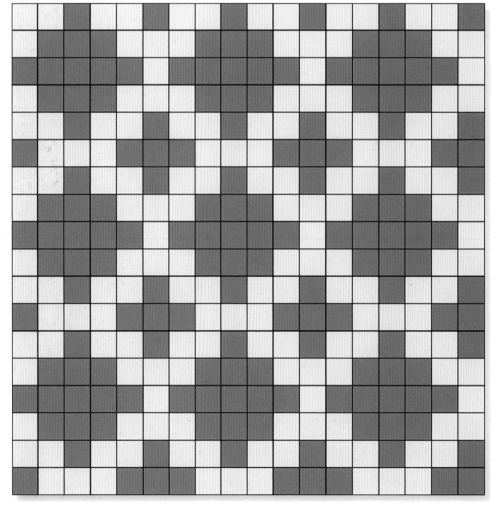

11.3 Star Windows 2

Very similar but more regimented than drawing 11.2, this striking design is found as a concrete window grille.

11.4 Iranian Interlocks

This very clever design is found on the walls of the Iranian Hospital in Dubai, U.A.E., as shown in the photo at right. Note how the dark blue and light blue patterns interlock perfectly. The design flows horizontally and can be continuously repeated in all directions.

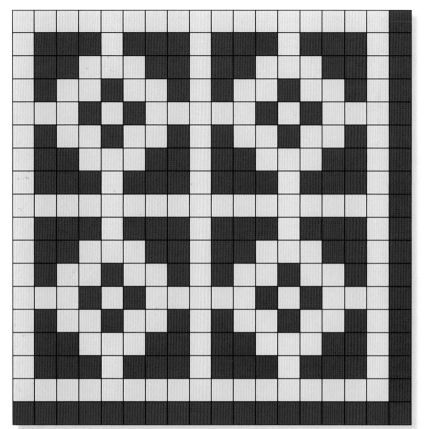

11.5 Whole-Square Diamonds

This is the whole-square version of tiled diamonds. It is found on a brick design in the Ibn Battuta Mall, Dubai, U.A.E., pictured below.

11.6 Omani Window

This striking design is simple yet fascinating. The alternating horizontal and vertical lines seem to rotate around the small central squares, with each square becoming the center of a spiral. When viewed from a distance, we imagine we see the lines weaving over and under one another. The pattern is found as a window grille in the famous Sultan Qaboos Mosque in Oman.

11.7 Blocked Spirals

This pattern is similar to, though not as sophisticated as, drawing 11.6. It was inspired by a concrete block wall, shown in the photo at left.

11.8 Large Diamond Checkerboard

Probably the most commonly seen whole-square design, this repeated diamond pattern comes in many variations and is easy to reproduce in tiles, as shown in the photo on the left.

11.9 Small Diamond Checkerboard

This is a simpler, more clear-cut version of a whole-square diamond pattern. The photo below right (of a mosque wall in Brunei) shows a tiled pattern that inserts the diamond into a larger collection of shapes.

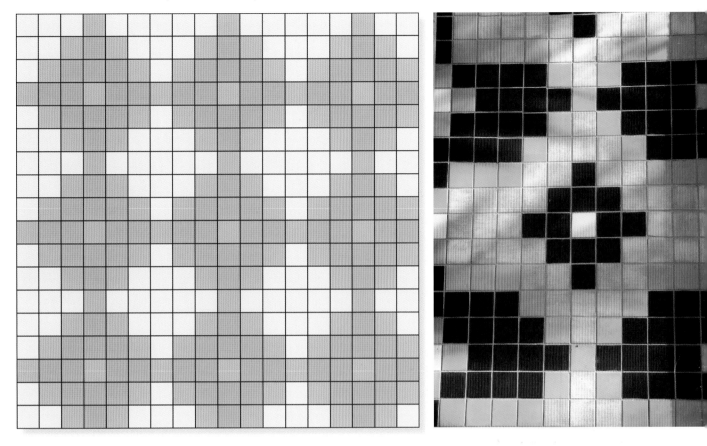

11.10 Long Diamond

This design was made by taking part of a design seen on a mosque wall (seen in the photo above right) and experimenting with repeating it on all four sides. The result is a pleasingly accentuated border around the diamond and a pattern that can repeat continuously in all directions.

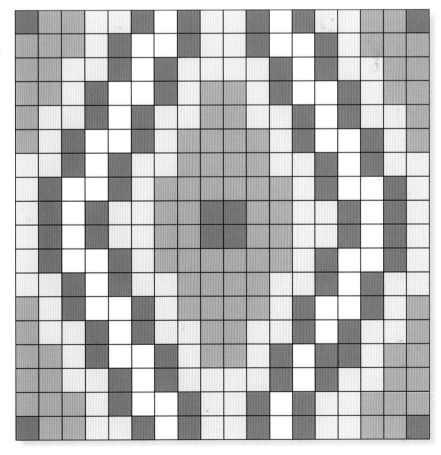

11.11 Adapted Diamonds

This design is found on a brick wall in a modern mall, shown in the photo below left. It has adapted the common whole-square diamond into a pleasing repeating pattern.

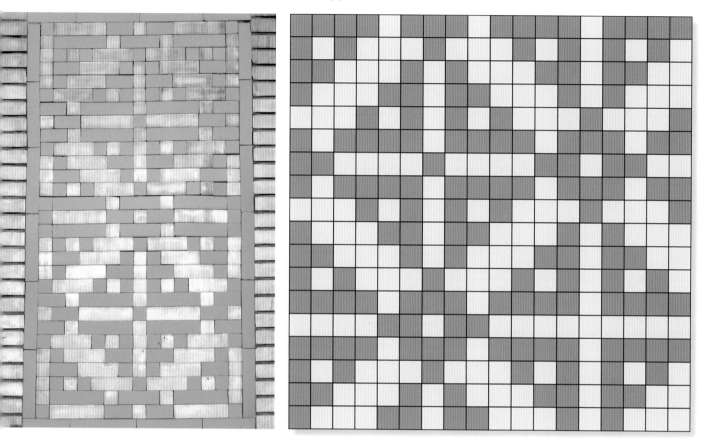

11.12 Big Flower

We can experiment with creating other shapes using whole square tiles. The patterns need to be simple and bold, like this flower.

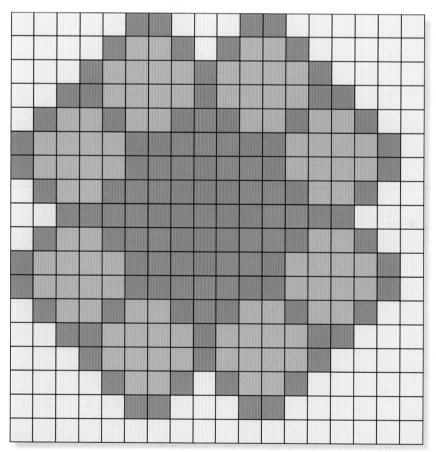

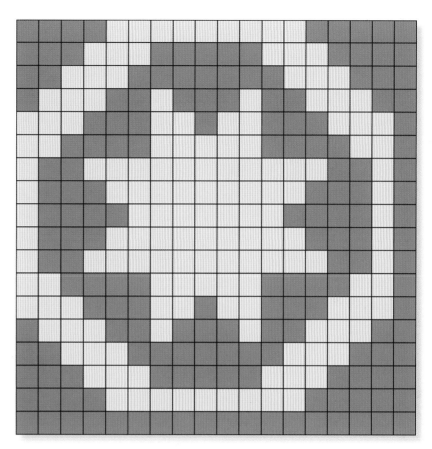

11.13 Big Star Medallion

Looking reminiscent of a badge or a flag design, this drawing shows how an eight-pointed star can be made with whole squares.

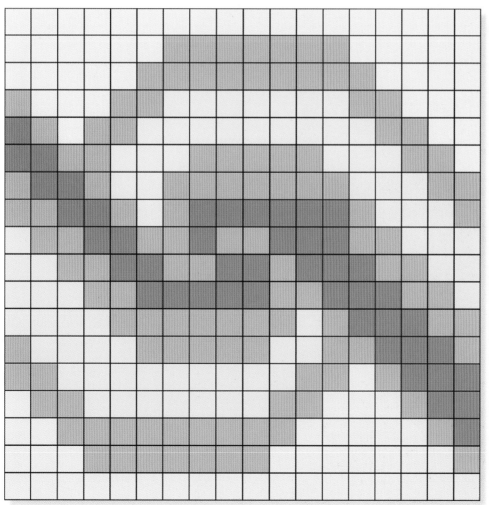

11.14 Big Wave

This "giant sea wave" design is another example of how effective a whole square pattern can be.

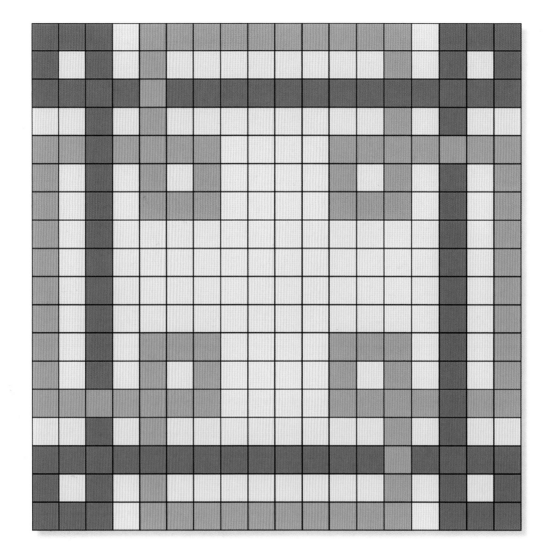

11.15 Dubai Border

Here we see another way to use whole squares, that of making an easy border around a central area. The woven effect gives added interest and is not difficult to achieve. Chapter 9 has more drawings such as this one. This design was found on a tiled wall in Dubai, U.A.E., as shown in the photo on the left.

11.16 Cross-Stitch Star

Inspired by a traditional cross-stitch design on a Palestinian blouse, pictured below right, this design translates into quite a dramatic whole-square tiling pattern.

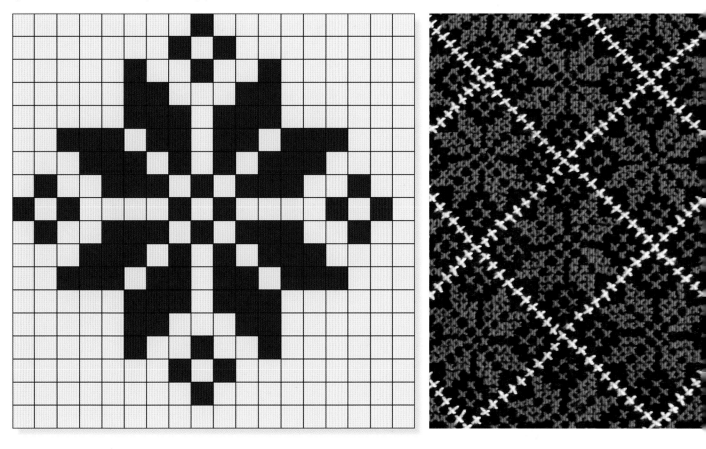

11.17 Iranian Mosaic

This striking design is found as a mosaic on the walls of a mosque in Iran.

11.18 Koru Sampler

The coiled fern frond design, called "koru" in New Zealand, is suited to whole-square designs. This drawing shows a number of different "curls," produced by an ever decreasing number of squares as you turn in a new direction. For example, in the top right-hand frond, the curl is made first by a line of five squares, then four, then three, then two, then one. Bigger fronds can be made by starting with a row of six squares, and so on. Children would enjoy walking around these curls on a tiled floor.

Fern frond patterns can be used as borders, easily coping with turning a square corner or framing something diagonally. Interestingly, if we extend the basic smaller curl into a long border, it becomes virtually identical to the classic Greek border. This gives us a hint of just how universal some geometric designs are.

Conclusion

Tiled floors and walls are a popular phenomenon. A tiled area does not need to be a bland space. The possibilities for using square tiles as a decorative medium are huge and largely untapped. All we need is a little "square thinking" to transform the geometric patterns we see in the world's cultures around us into beautiful tile designs.

Choosing to tile part of a home or workplace can suddenly make it take on a new dimension. Do you wish to create an atmosphere that echoes elements of your surroundings? Or choose an exotic style taken from distant lands? Perhaps you want to bring to mind a particular motif that has personal significance or emphasize a design feature being used in a nearby gate or curtain. Once the mind begins to work in this way, a whole new genre in interior and exterior decoration emerges.

Although the idea may be seldom utilized in today's modern world, older civilizations paid a lot of attention to permanent surface decorations in homes and public spaces. Skilled craftsmen were employed to carve or paint patterns, pictures and calligraphy that typically covered whole walls, both inside and outside buildings. From Egyptian hieroglyphics to European frescoes, the idea of putting designs on floors, walls and even ceilings has been around for a long time. Using modern tiles to achieve a similar effect is really just a fresh way of looking at an ancient practice.

The 11 chapters in this book provide a set of ideas and templates for such decorative tile work. The designs can be used as they are or varied and adapted. They may also provide the reader with a spark of inspiration to create their own original tiling design.

Happy tiling!

Blank square tile grids to copy and use to create your own designs.

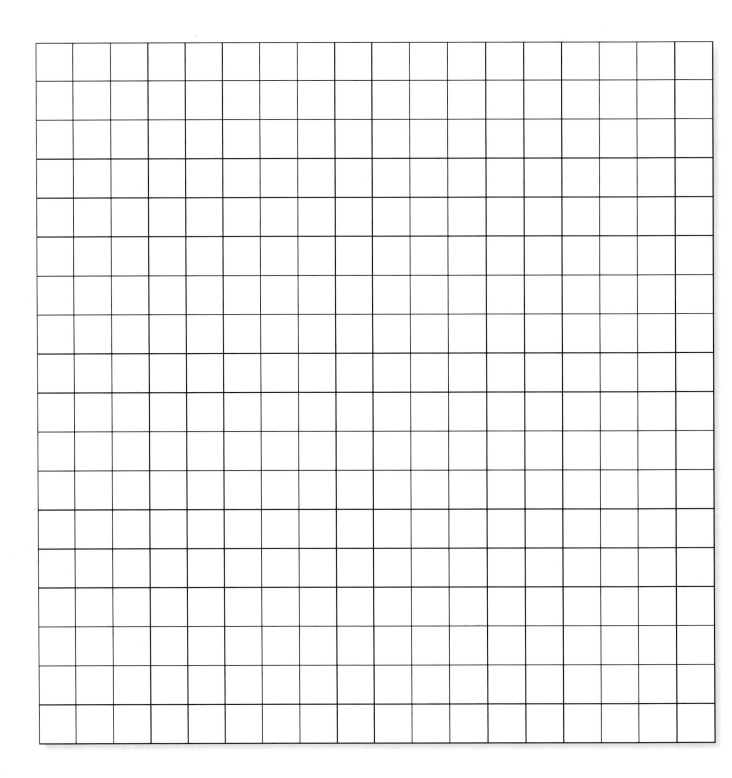

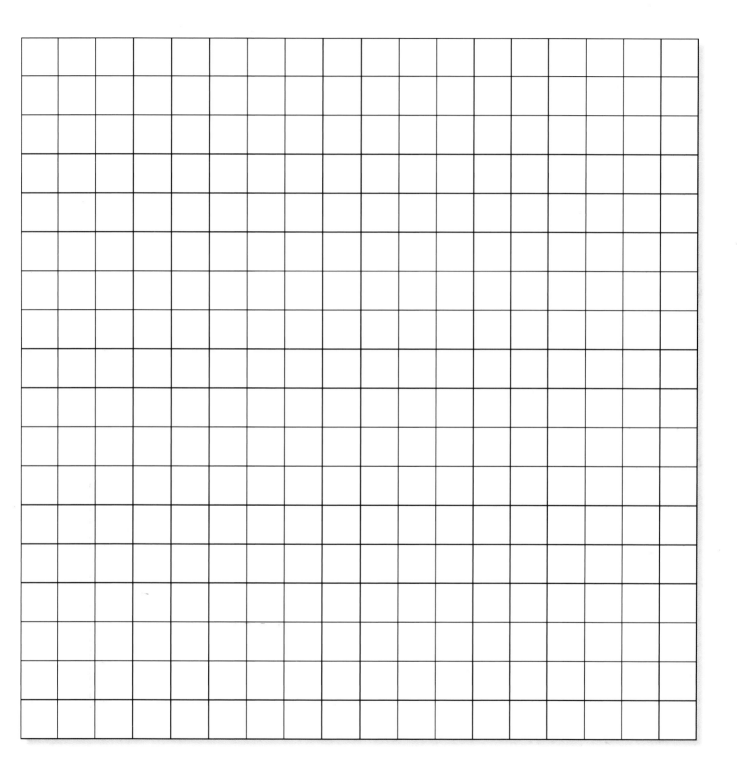

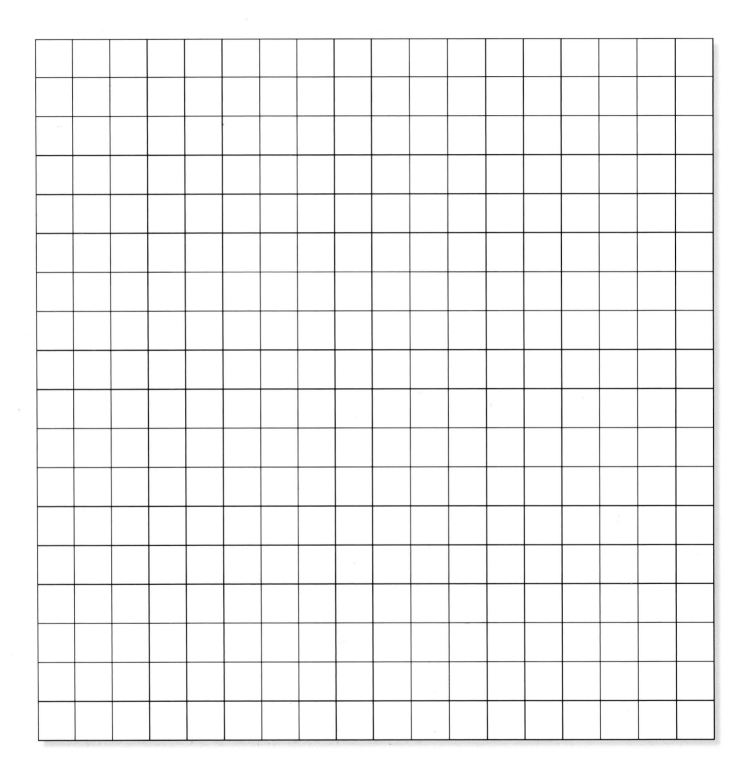